Letters from Togo

Singular Lives

The Iowa Series in North American Autobiography

Albert E. Stone, Series Editor

Letters from Togo

By Susan Blake

FOREWORD BY ALBERT E. STONE

University of Iowa Press 𝚿 Iowa City

University of Iowa Press, Iowa City 52242
Printed in the United States of America
First edition, 1991

Printed on acid-free paper

Library of Congress
Cataloging-in-Publication Data
Blake, Susan Louise, 1946–
    Letters from Togo/by Susan Blake;
foreword by Albert E. Stone.—1st ed.
      p.   cm.—(Singular lives)
    ISBN 0-87745-339-X,
    ISBN 0-87745-340-3 (pbk.)
    1. Lomé Region (Togo)—Description.
2. Blake, Susan Louise, 1946– —Jour-
neys—Togo—Lomé Region. 3. Lomé
Region (Togo)—Social life and customs.
4. Université du Bénin. 5. Blake, Susan
Louise, 1946– —Correspondence.
6. Literature teachers—Togo—Lomé
Region—Correspondence. 7. Literature
teachers—United States—Correspondence.
I. Title. II. Series.
DT582.9.L65B55   1991   91-20943
916.681—dc20   CIP

To my parents,
who made travel and letters
part of life

CONTENTS

Acknowledgments

I am grateful to the Fulbright Scholar Awards Program for the opportunity to teach in Togo, to the National Endowment for the Humanities for a year free to write, to the University of Iowa Center for Advanced Studies for a creative community and generous support services, and to Lafayette College for leave time and a summer research fellowship at crucial moments.

I would also like to thank all those who read these letters at various stages and asked me questions or answered mine. Particular thanks are due to Adalaide Morris and Frederic Will, whose perceptive criticism and encouragement made all the difference.

Foreword

Albert E. Stone

Letters from Togo, the fourth volume in the Singular Lives series, is a candid, perceptive, humorous account of one white woman abroad in contemporary Africa. It juxtaposes the familiar and the exotic to make a convincing portrait of its author, a teacher of American and African-American literature at a Pennsylvania college who is called on to play many roles—teacher, American, friend, social critic, single woman, enthusiastic traveler. As the wide-ranging record of an intense, mid-career academic's encounter with a foreign culture, thanks to a Fulbright visiting lectureship, *Letters from Togo* readily recalls the third autobiography in this series, Gary Gildner's *The Warsaw Sparks* (1990). The common theme of the midwestern poet and short story writer in Poland and the eastern scholar in Togo is creating a life and self in a radically different world. Their common resources for recreating themselves in unfamiliar settings are the memories, reflections, and dreams of a recent past. Their common challenge is to arrange these vivid outer and inner sensations into a narrative of encounters with the Other as a medium of self-definition.

What makes Blake's and Gildner's very topical narratives essentially autobiographical is the interplay in each text between immediacy and retrospection, between the striking scenes before us (often evoked by the present tense that Blake has wisely chosen) and the meanings which the passage of time and thoughtful reflection afford. In *Letters from Togo* the passing scene contains within it germs of later interpretation and generalization, as in the following representative impression:

> Whenever I turn onto the Route d'Atakpamé from the quiet *cité* I
> feel as though I'm jumping into a Woody Allen film—anything can
> happen, and whatever it is, I'm watching it and part of it at the same

time. A man pedals around the Rond Point, back straight, eyes front, balancing a kitchen table on his head. At the light at the Boulevard Circulaire, I pull up behind a chic woman on a motorcycle—long tight skirt hiked up over her knees, high heels hooked over the pedals, head encased in helmet. Without taking her eyes off the light, she reaches into her shoulder bag and tosses a coin to the beggar sitting on the corner.

Here as often elsewhere, Blake sits silently in her recently purchased Honda; she's the *yovo* (white) driver passing or watching both actors. But her presence is felt in the as-yet-undissected implications of the scene. Like the bicyclist, everyone in Lomé seems to know how to balance the equivalents of familiar household tables on their heads while negotiating city traffic. In this symbolic postcolonialist situation, the man on the bicycle stands for Mahouna, Blake's housekeeper, and even for René, her charming but fickle shorttime lover. All three men are cultural acrobats struggling within and between conflicting desires, roles, and ways of life. So, too, is the helmeted woman on the motorcycle. Her apparently cold modern chic coexists with her automatic gesture of generosity and underlines the central social insight Blake everywhere communicates: the endless permutations of have and have-not life in Lomé, Togo, Africa, the world.

Implicit, therefore, in this urban moment are issues of class, race, nationality, cultural change, and history that Susan Blake records so sensitively. Her insights differ from Gildner's because she is a woman, this is Africa not Eastern Europe, she hasn't baseball as a medium of cross-cultural communication. Yet like Gildner Blake lives in order to write and writes her autobiography in order to evaluate what she has lived. In the process, social experience and its analysis are inseparable from self-awareness, for Blake early realizes that the need to sustain half a dozen roles or even identities applies to herself as well as to her Togolese friends and colleagues.

What makes this thickening of cultural and psychological description possible is the network of personal relationships Blake develops and fuses into relived experiences by writing letters as autobiography. Moreover, unlike Gildner, who has his American girlfriend with him in Warsaw and welcomes a visit from his daughter and grandchild, Blake alights alone at the Lomé airport. Before playing the visiting professor, she must meet many new friends who prove essential to making sense of herself in a new world. Blake's narrative demonstrates over and over how adept she is at forming fruitful friendships. These are international and interracial and involve men and women of different generations. Both French and English are necessary for these modes of cross-cultural intercourse. Through her friends' problems and solutions as well as her own experiences, she learns how to move, think, and feel in necessarily new ways. Fresh insights into broadly human circumstances continually arise from this immersion in the small world of Lomé and the Togolese countryside. Often Blake learns simply by observation (as at the Rond Point). But more frequently education appears in and through daily conversations and evening get-togethers. "For a while I thought of these evenings as an escape from what I was really here for," she writes, "which was to get to know Togolese culture. Now I think they're part of the purpose. Because the interesting thing about living in Lomé is not simply Togolese culture, which we can never be part of anyway, but the intersections of different cultures, which include Bombay bourgeois, Cambridge counter, British colonial, and all the rest."

Typifying this mélange with its interactive, international consciousness is an evening at an African performing arts school for Europeans:

> Last night Nick ["Cambridge counter"] and Geeta ["Bombay bourgeois"] and I went to the graduation recital of a drumming and dancing school for Europeans run by Nick's Ghanaian master-drummer friend Mustapha and his German wife, Heide. At first it was just funny and embarrassing: seminaked whitefolks prancing around to the laughs and whistles of a Togolese audience. But the whistles signified admiration, and after awhile it was clear that two of the students were really good, even by African standards, and the rest had obviously learned a lot. . . .
>
> A spectacle like this makes you wonder who you are. We were European like the dancers but sitting in the audience, in judgment, like the Togolese. But none of us could have danced as well as the worst of these performers, so our judgment had more to do with how well they were representing us than how successfully they were imitating Togolese dancers. Nick was there as both kin to the performers—since he too is studying African music—and a colleague of their teacher. After the dancing, he played guitar with Mustapha's group in a demonstration of the fusion of African music and Western instruments.

Blake's private life echoes the range and emotional depths of such public insights. She must embrace similar complexities in relations with

René and the American exchange students from California, with the beggar
at the door and colleagues and students at the university. Watching by
living, living by watching both produce a political conclusion that is as
heartfelt as it is unexceptionable. Toward the end of her narrative she
summarizes the ideological lesson of Lomé:

> The good part of the small, interconnected world is the intercon-
> nectedness: the way Togolese and Americans meet at the airport for a
> community send-off; the way Amy and Rama can meet in SGGG [the
> European supermarket] and join forces to help their classmate from
> Chad; the way black, white, and *métisse* children form big frisbee
> games in the Sarakawa pool; the way their French, German, and
> American mothers meet and gab in whichever is the common lan-
> guage of the group; the way, freed from our own cultures, black and
> white Americans, U.S. Americans and Québecois, North Americans
> and Russians form new alliances and identities.

Yet these happy memories lead to a sober conclusion. "But all the cosmopolitanness that makes Lomé exciting comes from the same thing," she
observes.

> It's the fact that Togo is a poor country that brings aid workers from
> all over the world, creates the international atmosphere, and supports
> the restaurants, cultural centers, and supermarkets where we meet.
> There's no relationship—between teacher and student, between
> American and Togolese colleagues, between expatriates—that doesn't
> derive from the national and racial distinction between having and
> not having. And there's no gesture of the day that doesn't reflect it.
> Buying bread, taking out the garbage, getting into the freshly washed
> car, stopping at a light. When I go to the Sarawaka pool with Lee Ann
> and her kids, we spend about 4,000 francs to get in, while the guy
> who brings us pads for the lounge chairs probably makes 1,000 a day.
> What I'm looking forward to most in going home is being simply
> myself, not a *yovo,* not a fine lady, not a representative of the privileges
> to which others aspire.

But returning to Pennsylvania to resume being "simply myself" is no
longer possible and Blake knows that. "Of course, going home doesn't
change the basic relationship. It only puts it farther away."

Living a crucial year in Lomé hasn't been the sole source of this woman's education in who she really is. She is, as the preface announces, a scholar who's writing a monograph on British women who travel in and write about Africa. *Letters from Togo* therefore represents an interruption and an unexpected alternative to a more academic exercise. The eventual literary, cultural, and feminist study of earlier European women's experiences, though not yet completed, shadows this autobiography. In a sense, readers detect this subtext in the relatively infrequent literary allusions to authors like Isabella Bird and Mary Kingsley. Other readers and moviegoers may think they hear echoes of Isak Dinesen's classic *Out of Africa*. But that famous European-African encounter story, it seems to me, is much less germane to the postcolonialist education Susan Blake dramatizes than another book, Margery Perham's *African Apprenticeship*. Though Blake's story mostly rings ironic changes on the Oxford don's personal history, there are some inevitable continuities. Both narrate experiences in the form of letters. In 1929, Perham received a Rhodes traveling fellowship (not very different from a Fulbright). This brought her back to Africa, still the romantic dream of her girlhood and the memory of one earlier stay in British Somaliland. Blake, too, recalls reading novels and travel accounts. Both women feel the conflicting pulls of detached observation and immersion in what Perham thinks is the destructive element. Both dress for the part, eat and cook indigenous food, register domestic as well as political perceptions.

The differences between the eighties American and her twenties British antecedent are even more striking. Blake has confronted and discarded the racism, snobbery, and chauvinism which Perham so artlessly voices as concomitants of her fascination with and love of Africa. The two authors stand on opposite sides of the historic divide between colonialist and postcolonialist worlds. This chasm is nicely epitomized in the arrival scenes in *Letters from Togo* and *African Apprenticeship*. (Mary Louise Pratt in *Writing Culture* points out how crucial arrival scenes are in ethnographies, and it's clear the same holds true for many autobiographies.) "Landing in Lomé was like falling down the rabbit hole," Blake begins. "Six soporific hours on the plane—then down the stairs to heat, glare, noise, and color on fast forward. The woman in front of me swung her carry-on onto her head and strutted into the terminal. A crowd waved from the roof." An American colleague and the Togolese cultural affairs officer greet her and whisk "unmistakably American me" through customs. "The scene keeps shifting between the familiar and the bizarre."

More than half a century before, Perham wrote in her diary (later letters, finally autobiography) of arriving in Durban. Instead of a strutting African with her luggage on her head, Perham sees "kaffir" stevedores on the dock in earrings and filthy clothes, with impudent stares and unsettling laughter. "I seemed to feel the immensity of the problem they represented and the absurdity of my attempting to understand it," she confesses with a trepidation Blake never feels. "And this was only a sample, only the first corner of the continent which I could visualize spreading west and north, the whole terrifying map, with its enormous distances, its oppressions and cruelties, its voiceless primitive people, its senseless political divisions . . . I felt I dared not face this ridiculous enterprise." After this temporary revulsion, Perham goes ashore to confront Africa. She first interrogates a hard-nosed Scots manager who rehearses the stern racist rules under which the black stevedores labor. Their chat is interrupted by a policeman who reports the accidental death, a few minutes before, of a dockhand. He gives the manager the victim's still bloody belt and wallet. "The manager took them, excused himself from coming with me and shook hands. I withdrew mine to find it stained with the blood of No. 1102." Horror and a dimly perceived complicity in that horror are both recalled by the Englishwoman.

Though less dramatic and far less culturally doctrinaire than *African Apprenticeship*, *Letters from Togo* is an autobiography moving, however unintentionally, toward ethnography. Thus it reflects the truism among anthropologists that the best studies of foreign cultures not only are based on firsthand experiences of relatively circumscribed social settings but also draw upon repeated rather than single visits. Susan Blake reports two such subsequent visits to Togo. In August 1990, despite superficial changes in the economic situation, her Lomé friends still felt frustrated. Those whose local circumstances had improved still could not travel, while those who had since lived and studied abroad found that, upon their return, relatives and friends would not accept them as both Togolese and citizens of a wider world. "'You're back,' they'd say. 'I'm here,' he'd reply." As for the author, she says nothing about the difficulties of returning to Pennsylvania—a reticence regarding her non-African life that pervades this autobiography. Returning to Lomé, however, reminds her that even an American full of individualism is not free there to live out all the possibilities of autonomy and interconnectedness.

By January 1991, however, the democracy movement spreading across Africa, as it spread across Eastern Europe in 1989, had surfaced in Togo. There Blake finds the same friends who had been frustrated five months before suddenly energized, outspoken, and looking to the future. This gives her hope for both Africans and Americans. "I don't know what I'll find the next time I go to Lomé," she concludes, "but now I expect change and hope that change will continue to shrink the gulf of inequality." It is a characteristically guarded finale to a memoir by an American woman who guards her autonomy even as she opens herself generously to new realms of relationship and social reality.

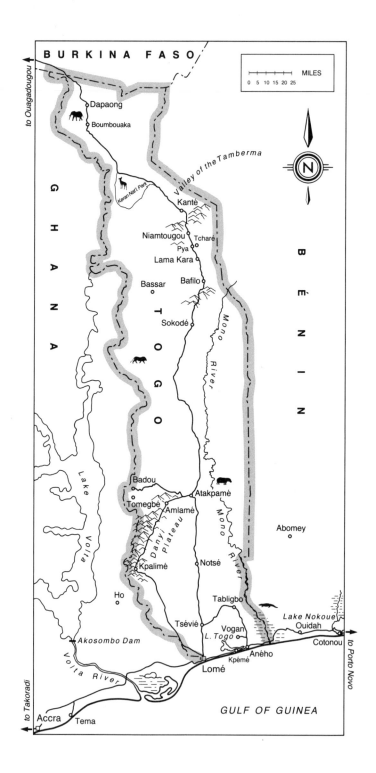

Preface

These are the letters I might have written from Togo had I had time and perspective. They're based on the letters I did write, but they've gone through some changes.

I went to Togo as a Fulbright lecturer in the fall of 1983 to teach American literature for a year at the University of Benin in Lomé. When I announced my plans, friends asked, "Where's Togo? Will it be primitive? Why *Togo?*"

Why Togo? Because I hadn't been there before. Because Togo was small, centrally located, and representative of West African culture. Togo had a little of all the African geographical features except desert. Its people, descendants of refugees from the aggressive kingdoms to the east and west, reflected the cultures of the whole Gulf of Guinea region. It had been touched by Christianity, Islam, and all the European colonial ventures, but it had not become Muslim like Senegal or Christian like Liberia, and the French didn't dominate as they were said to in Côte d'Ivoire. Like all African countries, Togo was poor, but its people were not starving. Like most, it was a military dictatorship, but not as openly repressive as some. The Togolese people had a reputation for friendliness. Lomé, the capital, was said to be a pleasant city without the high rises of Abidjan or the chaos of Lagos. And the university there maintained an apartment for the Fulbrighter, so I wouldn't have to start out by looking for housing. I had traveled in West Africa five summers before to see the world from which the African literature I had been reading came. I realized then that I couldn't "see" Africa by traveling through it. I would have to live there with a function in the society. The Fulbright exchange program offered an opportunity to live in Africa, and Togo seemed a good place to live. I wanted to experience Africa, but I knew that what I could grasp in a year was limited. Togo seemed to encompass African experience and yet to be compassable itself.

None of this satisfied. The real question was, "Why Africa?" I had none of the conventional reasons to go to Africa—roots to seek, research to pursue, a husband to accompany—so why go? I wanted to answer, "Why not?" I resented the question because it seemed restrictive. I suspected that it would not have been asked if I'd been black or asked in the same way if I'd been male or married or headed for Sweden.

I came to as much of an answer as I can give to "Why Africa?" as I thought about the question, "Will it be primitive?" This question meant, I think, "How will you whom we think we know live in a place we can't imagine?" This is the question I tried to answer in dense, detailed, almost daily letters home. I was working on it for myself as well as for others; I typed on self-copying paper from the French supermarket and kept a fattening file of letter copies. I realize now that to answer this question, to explore the experience of being a 'stranger, in effect to write those letters, was most of the reason I went to Togo.

When I went out to the mailbox the day after I returned from Togo, my next-door neighbor came over to say welcome home. I stepped forward and leaned into the anticipated handshake. He stopped a couple of feet away and put his hands in his pockets. I shuffled to regain my balance.

Another neighbor walked over from her mailbox and asked, "Do you feel as though you've been away a year?"

I had a sudden vision of what the year would have been like at home, slipping by in routine and, once past, indistinguishable from other years. How little different a summer day in 1984 would have felt from a summer day in 1983. Yes, I felt I'd been away a year, exactly a year, a real year, a year more real in its duration than any I could remember.

In the month before school started I tried, without success, to get some of the impact of the year down in writing. In January, between semesters, I tried again. I reread the letters I'd written from Togo; relived the heat, humor, boredom, anxiety, and exhilaration of the previous year; and made several writing starts. But each one dead-ended in what seemed a trivial but still insuperable problem. Like verb tense. The simple question of whether to write in past or present tense involved fundamental questions I couldn't answer. Where was I in relation to what I was telling? How much did I want to claim to know about things whose outline and implications had sunk in only gradually? How much did I know anyway? How did I feel about the sweaty person in the dark bedroom laboring over the tinny typewriter? Verb tense implies form. If I wrote in the past, was the work a narrative, in which the beginning is written with consciousness of the end? If I wrote in the present, was it a journal? Form implies audience. To whom was I writing? How much did I want to reveal?

I put the letters away and turned to other things.

Three years later, the need to write about Togo returned. I was at the University of Iowa, on leave from teaching at Lafayette College, to work on a study of white women's African travel narratives. As I read other travelers' narratives, episodes, images, even paragraphs of my own experience kept interrupting me. As I read Esther Warner's account of settling into a company house on the Firestone plantation in *New Song in a Strange Land*, I heard Mahouna lecturing me about keeping the door locked, myself trying to describe insulated staples to hardware clerks. Miss M. Gehrts's *Camera Actress in the Wilds of Togoland* brought back the Kabyé hills and the young woman who'd walked a hundred kilometers from Bassar to the Tcharé market to buy a water jar. *The Prophet's Camel Bell*, Margaret Laurence's reflective account of a sojourn in British Somaliland in the 1950s, revived that fist in the pit of the stomach that clenched when I caught a glimpse of myself as the memsahib, the innocent, ignorant liberal. I would find my-self staring into space, the book in my lap, silently recounting, replay-ing, debating these scenes from Togo. I took to outlining on bookmarks. The details filled in as I took walks and swam laps. When a couple of episodes had formed in my mind, I took time out from "my work" to write them down.

The problem of form and tense had taken care of itself. The episodes took the form of letters, written at a specific moment within the experience about moments in the recent past. Letters, as opposed to a narrative, preserved the process of discovery I had gone through and, I realized later, allowed it to continue. I wondered that I hadn't thought of letters from the beginning since letters were my sources and had always been what I wrote for myself.

Why was my experience in Togo reasserting itself after three to four years of dormancy? Partly, no doubt, because I had time. Partly because the travel narratives I was reading dealt with the same problems of adaptation I'd faced. Partly because I was facing them again. Though Iowa was much closer to home than Togo had been, to my eastern eyes it offered cultural curiosities with which I larded letters home: bicycle routes shared with

Amish buggies, potential presidents speaking in university classrooms, grad students in Guatemalan shawls mixing with farmers in seed-corn hats at the Wednesday-night auction. Once again, I had set up a temporary home in an intense rush. Once again, I was learning a new environment and making new friends. Some of them asked about Togo, some with the idea of teaching in Africa themselves, giving me the opportunity to re-tell—and rethink—stories already old at home. Perhaps another reason Togo was intruding, I feared, was that a new scholarly project was hard; memory was easier than analysis.

I didn't write the letters in this volume in chronological order, but the emotional progress of their writing followed loosely that of the year in Togo. The episodes that took shape in the fresh fall days when a year of leave stretched ahead and everything seemed possible were based on the upbeat letters about getting satisfactorily settled in the first exhilarating weeks in Togo. In January, when the Iowa winter settled in, and my leave was half over, and I wasn't sure what I'd have to show for it, I wrote "The Doorbell," the first of these letters that wasn't based on a letter written in Togo. I'd thought a lot about the beggars who came to the door, but I hadn't written about them. The subject was too distressing; I didn't know what I thought of my own reactions. It was about January, too, in Togo, when the heat was getting hotter and the newness had worn off, that I began to realize Togo wasn't as accessible as I'd believed at first and to feel the ambivalence and stress of being a Westerner in the Third World. When "The Doorbell" took shape, I knew that what I was doing was not indulging in nostalgia but going through a new experience. I began to admit that it was "my work."

As I wrote, I kept running into things I didn't remember or never knew, questions I hadn't asked. What was the name of the sour fruit Véronique kept pushing on me? What is the linguistic relationship between Ewe and Mina? Why did voodoo novices go topless? I looked for books on African religions in the University of Iowa library, sent lists of questions to Togolese friends, and wondered why I hadn't remembered or learned or asked these things on the spot. One reason, I realized, is that knowing them didn't seem important in Togo; getting along was enough to manage. Another reason is that writing is different from absorbing. Writing demands names for things apprehended by sight or smell or a feeling in the pit of the stomach. It requires specific contexts and causes for vague impressions and fragmentary memories. It implies control, far more control than I felt in Togo.

So these letters, written and rewritten in Iowa City and Easton, with the contributions of scholars, of earlier travelers, and of many readers, both American and Togolese, reflect my distance from Togo now as well as my life there seven years ago.

1983

Arrival

⊠ ⊠ ⊠

Landing in Lomé was like falling down the rabbit hole. Six soporific hours on the plane—then down the stairs to heat, glare, noise, and color on fast forward. The woman in front of me swung her carry-on onto her head and strutted into the terminal. A crowd waved from the roof.

Everything has gone right. Unmistakably American Lee Ann Adamah, the English Department member who wrote to me over the summer, and Simon Amégavie, the top Togolese officer at the American Cultural Center, picked out unmistakably American me before I got through the passport control line and called over the customs barrier that they'd meet me at the exit with a porter. The customs inspector passed over my forty rolls of film (ten times the duty-free allowance) and questioned my contact lens solutions. Simon persuaded the stone-faced security police officer in the airport to let me declare my typewriter today instead of leaving it and coming back for it "tomorrow." The water and electricity were on in my apartment, Martin the houseboy was busy cleaning, and, despite my predecessor Flint's assurance that I wouldn't see them before Christmas, all the boxes of books I'd sent were neatly stacked in the bedroom. Simon had brought them over this morning. The scene keeps shifting between the familiar and the bizarre. One minute I'm typing ten copies of a paragraph on monkey hunting in Togo in upper and lower case under a policeman's glare; the next, I'm looking at my own name in my own handwriting on the boxes I last saw in my own office at Lafayette.

From the apartment, we drove downtown to the American Cultural Center. The first stretch of road was a new four-lane divided highway with sidewalks and streetlights. "The president is your neighbor," explained Simon. Then the road narrowed past a taxi park and market and the red clay itself seemed to spring to life. Stacks of cans, fruits, and baguettes spilling over the curb; motorcycles weaving between bicycles and taxis; women wrapped in jewel-tone prints shuttling across the road under basins of freight; horns, shouts, smoke, and exhaust mingling in the air; everything glowing in the late afternoon sun. Lomé is no transplanted European city; it's more like an overgrown village, where life is lived on the street.

At the cultural center, Simon went off to collect me an embassy welcome kit (a couple of cartons of household equipment) and Lee Ann led me through a dark chilly room where Peter Jennings was reading last month's ABC news to a tiny, chillier office where Kay Goode was waiting for us. Kay, a white-haired, chain-smoking Vermonter, is the regional English teaching officer, which means she supervises the teaching of English in the American cultural centers in several Francophone African countries. She beamed at me as if I were her favorite niece come to visit. "You don't *know* how we miss cultivated people here," she said, which makes me wonder what she expects. Lee Ann got us all Nescafé with Coffeemate and tried to explain to me what everyone in the center does, but I didn't absorb much of it, and I was glad when Simon came back with my welcome kit and Kay stood up and said, "I bet you'd like to go shopping."

She and Lee Ann took me to SGGG ("ess-twah-zhay," for Société Générale du Golfe de Guinée), a sort of Sears-cum-supermarket and apparently social center for the expatriate community. From the moment we got out of the car in the parking lot, we kept meeting people Kay and Lee Ann knew—Peace Corps volunteers, English teachers, parents of children who go to school with Lee Ann's kids, and an English Department colleague, Elise da Silva, who has invited Lee Ann and me to her house tomorrow. I even saw someone I knew: a French woman who made herself conspicuous in the departure lounge of Charles de Gaulle this morning by yelling at her four-year-old; but she didn't acknowledge me.

Between introductions, I went up and down the aisles pulling things off the shelves. The first aisle had the liquor. When I started with a bottle of Dutch gin and half a dozen cans of Schweppes tonic, Lee Ann and Kay looked at each other and said, "Our kind of woman, she has her priorities straight." Then, boxes of orange juice and long-life milk, cans of lentils, tomatoes, tuna from the Ivory Coast, duck and rabbit pâté from France, 250-gram tins of Nescafé, plastic boxes of peanut butter and pineapple-papaya preserves.

"If you have Africans cooking for you," said Lee Ann, "they're fussy about tomato paste and this is the right kind."

"Don't forget bug spray," said Kay.

The best thing was that I needed everything and didn't know how much anything cost. Lee Ann told me to divide the CFA price by four to get the price in cents (that is, there are 400 francs CFA to the dollar), but the dollar price in a different context doesn't mean much, and it was more fun not to know—one never-to-be-repeated moment of complete greedy freedom.

As we stood in the check-out line, an American voice cut through the general hum and clatter. "Hey, you guys, I hear English!" Around the end of the aisle sailed a tall black woman with thick brown braids hanging down her back and three limp-looking young white women in tow. "Do you know where they have popcorn?" she asked. They are students from California taking a junior year abroad in Togo. They said they arrived yesterday after two days of travel including a night in the Lagos airport. Only their leader looked recovered.

As we left the store, I asked Lee Ann how much to tip the man who was pushing my grocery cart across the parking lot. She said, "This is a big order, you could give him a hundred francs." When I got to the car, Kay had already given him 300.

My plane landed at two o'clock this afternoon. It's now eight. When Kay dropped me off about six, it was already getting dark. I put the perishables in the fridge and opened a can of tuna for supper. In another minute I'm going to spread the embassy sheets on the bed and crash. The apartment feels cavernous. The windows are black and bare, the ceilings high, and the lamplight doesn't reach into the corners. The air is still and close and filled with the buzz of cicadas. I'm just realizing that the throb I hear under the buzz must be drumming. Paris this morning seems years ago.

Clear Light of Day
✉ ✉ ✉ ✉ ✉ ✉

Things looked different this morning after a sweaty night sunk in a foam rubber mattress on sagging springs. I'm sure the drumming kept up till the birds took over.

This apartment is a two-story townhouse in a block of six in a gardened development built by the Caisse Nationale pour la Securité Sociale as a source of income. Most of the residents are foreigners. It's called the "Résidence du Bénin," but Simon and Lee Ann referred to it as the *cité*.

The bedroom, bath, and *cabinet* (toilet cubicle) are downstairs; the living and dining areas and kitchen upstairs. The Togolese, Simon Amégavie told me yesterday, find this arrangement as bizarre as the Americans do. They believe the bedrooms should be upstairs where it's cooler (because of the breezes through the treetops) and safer from intruders. The only windows are on the front and back, and on the first floor they're just transoms so the bedroom is dark. Because Americans have lived here before, the windows have screens. The dining room window looks out into a tree, full this morning of the bright yellow birds that got me up, and beyond to the street, where you can just barely see a couple of the one-story "villas" behind palm and rubber trees. The living room windows look out into coconut palm fronds. All the rooms, except the living room, which is open to the stairwell, have doors with locks and old-fashioned skeleton keys.

In the living room, a sofa and four armchairs, cheap Danish modern in teak with foam cushions covered in a faded red print, are arranged in a rectangle around a formica-topped coffee table. Tacked to the kitchen door is a dusty, yellowed kitchen towel printed with a map of Togo. At the other end of the kitchen, a door covered with a violent red cowboy poster screaming "USA" leads to a utility room, with laundry tubs, the water heater, wire clotheslines, and an assortment of mops and rags. The furniture,

Simon explained, dates from the days when the apartments were rented furnished. The appliances were provided—several Fulbrighters back—by the embassy. The furnishings are an accumulation of embassy welcome kits and Fulbrighters' contributions.

Yesterday I noticed the apartment's high ceilings, the teak beams criss-crossing the living room ceiling like a Japanese screen, the American refrigerator, the Ethan Allen chest in the bathroom. This morning I saw that one whole wall of the apartment, upstairs and down, is discolored from a leak in the roof. The leak has been fixed, but not the wall. Sheets of paint are flaking off the wall onto the living room couch and the kitchen counter. The knobs on the doors of the cupboards below the kitchen counter came off in my hand; the nuts holding them on have worked through the rotting wood. The cupboards have no shelves and no floor; the bottom of the cupboards is the cement floor of the kitchen. Tiny ants were crawling over the counter and under the cellophane of an unopened package of cookies in my box of groceries. The faucets in the laundry tubs and kitchen sink drip. All the dining room chairs wobble. The formica top is lifting off the table. When I opened the door of the closet under the stairs, mouse-size cockroaches fled. The closet is full of more broken chairs, damp cardboard boxes, and the overpowering essence of mildew.

I found the dishes and kitchen utensils in cupboards under the windows in the living room—the dishes (beige plastic) covered with dust, the dishtowels spread out under them mildewed. In another section of the living room cupboards are piles of books and pamphlets: a couple of Ewe grammars, *The Age of Innocence, Highlights of American Literature*, mysteries, *Europe on $5 a Day*, the *Peace Corps Medbook*—all mildewed. There are mildewed sheets on shelves in the bedroom closet, sprinkled with what looks like mouse droppings, and mildewed towels in the drawers of the Ethan Allen chest. The bathroom sink has separate hot and cold water faucets and no stopper. The tub stopper doesn't fit the sink. When I turned on the shower, nothing happened. I brought the showerhead (on a flexible pipe, European style) down into the tub and got a drizzle. It took half an hour for the drizzle to run warm. I "took a shower" squatting in the tub and holding the showerhead as low as possible—glad I got my hair cut before I came, wondering how you wash mildew out of sheets and towels in a drizzle.

Over breakfast, I perused a leaflet called "Housekeeping in the Tropics" from the pile of mimeographed notices and embassy directives in the living room cabinets. To combat damp, this Foreign Service Heloise advises, do not use wire hangers; they'll rust on your clothes. To prevent mildew, keep a light bulb burning in the closet, but be careful that it doesn't touch any of the clothes, or it may start a fire. Mothballs also help prevent mildew and have the additional merit of repelling cockroaches, which will eat your clothes.

Right then I started a list for the housewares and hardware departments of SGGG: mothballs, plastic hangers, sink stopper, washers for the kitchen cupboard doors. Then a list for a carpenter: Glue table top and chairs; make bedboard; install shelves in kitchen cabinets; build bookcase.

The doorbell rang. Two women wanted to know if I had any work for them to do. Yesterday, when we dropped my luggage at the apartment, Simon Amégavie asked me when I wanted Martin to come this morning. I didn't think I wanted him to come at all. He had supposedly finished cleaning, and I thought I'd like time alone to put things away. "You'd better have him come," said Simon. So to be agreeable but give myself time to reconnoiter in private, I said, okay, how about ten o'clock. But it was barely eight and I couldn't put anything away until all the cupboards were scrubbed and aired, and when Martin came he'd have to ride his bicycle downtown to pay the overdue electric bill I'd found under the door. I'd been about to wash the dusty dishes under the drizzle in the lower-than-standard sink (the kitchen counters are table height and the table is counter height). Should I let them do something? Was it dangerous to let strangers into the house? The cautious Flint had said he'd given people odd jobs. These women looked okay. So I said, "Well, yes, you can wash some dishes." One washed, the other dried. I didn't know quite what to do myself. I wanted to clean the bedroom closet so I could put clothes away, but I didn't want to let strangers far out of my sight. On the other hand, I didn't want to stand over them. I started going through the mildewed books in the living room.

When they'd finished, I was relieved. I gave them each a hundred francs. At the door, the older one said, "Madame, you need a maid? I can clean; I can cook. I will come back tomorrow?"

"No," I replied, feeling stupid not to have realized that this was the point and trapped, too, because I might rather have a woman work for me but I really have no choice. "I have someone; I just needed a little extra help this morning."

"You will need some extra help again?" At this, Martin wheeled up on his bicycle, and the two women retreated.

Martin was not pleased. "Ça je n'aime pas," he said, shaking his head, "non, pas du tout." I should never let strangers into the house. They might have been staking it out to rob. And besides, this was his job. How did I think it made him feel to see strangers doing his job? And if something turned up missing, wouldn't I blame him? If I needed something I should ask him. I was the one who had said don't come until ten.

So, by ten o'clock in the morning on my first full day in Togo, I'd already offended the person I most need to get along with. I tried to explain that I had had no idea how much work there would be, that while maybe it hadn't been the best idea to let the women in, they had done a good job, hadn't done any harm, and hadn't taken anything away from him, that I wouldn't do it again, and that now that he was here we would see how much needed to be done and how often he should come.

This seemed to work, but it raised the question of hours and pay that Martin is anxious to settle and I want to postpone. How do I know how much time it will take to keep down the dust and ants, boil the drinking water, do the laundry, and I don't even know what else? Or what the going rate is, or even how much I can stand to have another person in the house? Flint's experience here is useless because he ate beans out of a can standing up in the kitchen and had Martin come only two mornings a week. I told Martin frankly that I didn't know what I would need, that I was used to taking care of my own house, but conditions were different here. I asked him if he'd like to learn to cook, told him I hoped he'd help me with my French, said, yes, I'd teach him some English. We agreed that he would come every day next week while I settle in, then we'd see about the future. By the time he left to pay the electric bill, we were co-conspirators in the protection of the apartment against mildew, strangers, and the electric company. But I hope I haven't promised too much.

All this happened before eleven o'clock. As Martin pedaled off, Lee Ann drove up to take me to Elise's to meet Dagadou, the department chair.

On the way, Lee Ann broke the news that she's leaving the English Department; she's accepted a job at the American International School, teaching fifth grade, at double her university salary. Lee Ann has five children; her husband, who is Togolese, is a chicken farmer, and the farm is apparently an unreliable source of income. She has been supporting the family on a salary of about $5,000 a year. And that salary is not secure, because the university is beginning to insist that professors have a doctorate, and Lee Ann has only a master's and sees no way to get a doctorate. No wonder she has snapped up the chance of $10,000. But she feels she has betrayed me, her colleagues at the university, the students, her intellectual aspirations, and, especially, her voluntary exile from the United States. She is embarrassed that it is the *American* School. She rationalizes that her Togolese circumstances require her to accept a better salary, but that while she will teach at the American School, she won't send her children there, although as a faculty member she could send them for free, while she pays tuition at the private Togolese schools they attend, which is one reason she needs the higher American School salary.

Lee Ann's departure worsens a staff shortage in the English Department. She won't be replaced; neither will a couple of Togolese members who have gone to the United States for graduate study. I am supposed to teach two courses for the C1 ("say-uhn," for first certificate, meaning third-year specialization) in American literature and one other that hasn't been decided yet. Lee Ann doesn't want to let go of her role in the department; she thinks I should be given the second-year introduction to British and American literature, not "wasted" on a first-year course. And she tells me to be sure I don't let Dagadou give me more than three courses.

Elise's house is on the Route de Kpalimé ("pahl-ee-may"), one of the main routes that lead out of central Lomé like the spokes of a wheel. Lee Ann parked next to one of the little bridges over the open sewer alongside the road. Handpainted on Elise's wooden gate is a sign advertising ice in three bowl-shaped sizes for 10, 25, and 50 francs and *yé-yé*, yogurt, for 50 francs—her daughter's and niece's little business, Elise explained. A cement walk leads across the yard of packed dirt, with a matted patch of grass here and there, to the house. In the yard are a mango and a papaya tree, a hibiscus, a few other flowering shrubs, and clotheslines. In a shed on the left, the washman was ironing with an iron he reheated on a charcoal fire. Two wooden chairs with cushions sit under the window on the porch. Pots of struggling spider plants and aloe line the edge. The window has bars on the outside, wooden shutters on the inside, no glass. The gray-painted cement floor of the porch continues inside. In front of the entrance, four heavy overstuffed chairs and a sofa covered in deep blue velour are grouped around a rectangular coffee table in the same arrangement I found in my apartment. On the right, in front of the door to the kitchen, which Elise quickly closed, is a rectangular table with half a dozen straight, flat-seated wooden chairs. On a chest in the corner, a portable television; on an end table by the sofa, a picture of Elise's two children in Nigerian costume and a professional portrait photo of Elise. Over them, on the wall, hang a crucifix and a calendar with a picture of Huck and Jim rafting down the Mississippi.

Elise greeted us with a handshake. Dagadou was already there. We arranged ourselves around the coffee table. Elise took orders for beer, Coke, and Fanta and passed saucers of peanuts her mother had roasted. The topics of conversation were familiar—the staff shortage in the English Department and the administration's lack of vision—but the details of those topics showed some of the ways in which teaching at a struggling African university is different from teaching at a private college in the U.S. One example of lack of vision on the part of the *directeur* of the Ecole des Lettres was his refusal to allocate money for the English Department to send someone to the University of Ibadan in Nigeria to buy books. If the allocation were given just once, the department could sell the books to the students and use the proceeds to keep up a stock. The *directeur* didn't openly refuse the request, of course; he just kept saying it was the *recteur*'s decision, when everybody knew the *recteur* didn't deal with such small matters.

Lee Ann's departure and my arrival led to the question of how to cover the American literature courses (though Dagadou said it was too early to make any decisions; classes don't start till the middle of October), and that led to a discussion of Miss Messan, the Togolese teacher of Afro-American literature. "She is difficult, really difficult," acknowledged Dagadou. "It's best not to cross her, but it's difficult, too. You'll see." A political appointment, he intimated. No one liked her, the students complained about her constantly, but the department couldn't get rid of her. Another strike against the *directeur* was favoritism toward her.

No one blamed Lee Ann for leaving. Elise and Dagadou knew you couldn't support a family on a university salary. They are both moonlighting to make ends meet. And they didn't think of her turning to an American institution as a betrayal. As far as they're concerned, I think, Lee Ann is American and would be a fool not to take advantage of what being American offers. Elise had all of her higher education in the States, culminating in a Ph.D. in linguistics from Michigan. Dagadou has done graduate work at Northwestern and hopes to return on a Fulbright grant next year to complete a Ph.D. They have no illusions about the romance or virtue of self-deprivation. Only Lee Ann believes in the ideals she thinks she is betraying.

From Elise's Lee Ann and I went to Kay's for lunch. Even after less than twenty-four hours in Togo, her house was a shock. The living area is on the second floor, over a utility room, a carport, and a terrace. When we opened the door at the top of the stairs, cool air hit, and we stepped into the U.S.A. A loden-green-and-gold color scheme, carpet over the tile floor, upholstered chairs back in the corners with baskets of *New Yorkers* beside them rather than pulled up close to the coffee table in front of the sofa, heavy drapes, pictures on the walls, Chopin on the stereo, bookshelves, plants—a room enclosed, solid, clean, a refuge from the heat and dust of the street below.

The table was set with things from Kay's family home—a white cloth and napkins embroidered with wildflowers, English china plates, pale blue wineglasses. Shuffling around the table in a white T-shirt stretched over his ample stomach and khaki pants sagging below, Clarence the cook looked a little out of place. But Clarence's comfort is really part of the comfort of the place. Cooking and cleaning (not much of that, Kay complained) for a single woman of plain tastes and generous instincts is a sort of retirement for Clarence, who once cooked for the Ghanaian ambassador. He has the time to try new recipes and sit in the shade with Koffi, the daytime *gardien*, and the freedom to plan the menus, determine the amounts, and dispose of the leftovers. His ability to speak English, cook American, and plan for large parties enables Kay, who speaks labored French, dislikes African food, and entertains prodigiously, to relax in her own home.

Kay applauded Lee Ann's decision to quit the university, too, but for reasons different from Elise's and Dagadou's. She and Lee Ann took up what I gather is their ongoing argument. Kay is a shameless chauvinist who can't believe that any American could take Africa seriously. She's extremely kind to individuals (a neighbor's houseboy, for example, who has been left without income while the neighbor is on leave) but the climate, conditions, culture, and institutions fill her with exasperation. In her living room she has stools from Thailand and paintings by her students in Poland, but nary a basket or handwoven napkin from Togo. Lee Ann married an African and insists that she doesn't like America, doesn't support American values, doesn't want her children growing up on TV and junk food. Kay can't believe that Lee Ann means what she says. "But Lee *Ann*," she says, "you're an *American*, you *love* your country, you *know* you do." These two could hardly be more squarely opposed on basic issues, but they seem to be devoted friends. It looks like they're both going to be my friends, too.

Lee Ann gave me her course materials for the second-year British and American literature course she thinks I should teach. They're not much, mostly mimeographed copies of poems by Keats, Shelley, Frost, and Poe. Lee Ann left the U.S. in the mid-1960s, fed up with the Vietnam War and what she considered a superficial, materialistic society. She missed the revolution in literary studies, the "discovery" of black and ethnic and women writers, the challenges to the literary canon, the connection of art and politics. She's teaching literature the way it was taught to her in a world she rejected. She's greedy for information on what's current, but she doesn't understand why there should have been a sea change. How do you catch somebody up on twenty years of political and intellectual change?

The help Kay offered is more practical. I'm to take my laundry to her house and pay Koffi to do it in the machines. This gesture seems to be quintessential Kay: spontaneous generosity that will help an American live up to standard and help "poor little Koffi" earn a little extra money.

Buying a Car
✉ ✉ ✉ ✉ ✉

This week I learned how to take taxis. The *cité* is four or five miles north of town, and the embassy people made me think it would be next to impossible to get taxis out here. Tuesday (Monday was Labor Day, the embassy's private holiday) Kay had the Cultural Center car pick me up so I'd be sure to arrive in time for my courtesy appointment with the ambassador. Wednesday I followed embassy advice and sent Martin out to the Route d'Atakpamé on his bicycle to bring a taxi into the *cité*. The fare was 500 francs, and I felt ridiculous. Thursday, Martin and I both walked out to the main road, carrying bundles of sheets and towels to be laundered at Kay's; this time the fare was 400. Thursday afternoon I returned by taxi with the carpenter and plumber that Patrice (the Togolese supervisor of maintenance on the embassy houses) got to help me fix up the apartment. They had to make a preliminary visit to see what needed to be done and how to get here. With John the carpenter negotiating, the fare was 350. Simon Amégavie had told me the fare from the *cité* to town should always be less than from town out because a taxi driver had less chance of getting a fare. This morning I walked out to the Route d'Atakpamé by myself and told the driver I never paid more than 300. He told me to hop in. The Togolese fare is 200, but it's accepted that *yovos* (whitefolks) pay more.

What I was doing in town all week was shopping for a car. I didn't find one until I'd passed the taxi test. To buy a car, you put the word that you want one on the grapevine and check out the notices on the bulletin board at Marox, the German grocery on the sea road about half a mile from the Cultural Center. Here outgoing expatriates pass on their cribs and air conditioners and cars to newcomers. I worked out the code for car ads ("*climatisée*," air conditioned; "break," station wagon; "*dédouanée*," tax already paid), copied down the information on three possibilities, and hiked back to the Cultural Center to call. At ten in the morning, even a half-mile walk is an undertaking. You can feel the sun sucking up the moisture from the last night's rain. Although most people walk, there is no accommodation for pedestrians—no sidewalks, no crossing lights. You walk in the sand along the irregular edge of the pavement—dodging puddles; garbage piles; tables stacked with oranges, Marlboros, and chewing sticks; mopeds; bicycles; and other pedestrians under headloads like ships under sail.

Back at the Cultural Center, damp and gritty, I perched on the edge of Sylvestre's desk to telephone. I'd rehearsed the opening line for my telephone debut in French, but forgot it when my first call was answered, "Hôtel de la Paix, bonjour." Since most people don't have private phones, they use company phones for private business. Two of the cars had been sold in June; the other turned out to be a truck.

Meanwhile, everyone I've met got into the act. Simon Amégavie had two friends with cars for sale; he'd get in touch with them. He also advised me to see his brother at the Renault dealership; sometimes new car dealers had used cars, too. Philippe Ekoué, a friend of Kay's I met at her house Sunday evening, knew someone selling a nice small Peugeot. Mac Macdowell, the joint administrative officer at the embassy, said he'd call one of his Togolese tennis partners, the service manager at the Honda dealership, who'd said he was fixing up a Civic for sale. Mac's an easy-going black ex-marine who takes almost subversive pleasure in his job of making Americans comfortable, more comfortable perhaps than they imagined they could be, in Africa. He was in his element bringing his Togolese and American friends together to help a woman buy a car.

Simon's brother at the Renault dealer turned out to be not a salesman but a bookkeeper; he introduced me to a salesman, who asked me to wait for a few minutes in the showroom while he finished with another customer, a huge woman impressively robed in a purple-and-green print looking at a top-of-the-line model. She had to be a "Nana Benz," one of the women who have gotten rich in the cloth trade, even if she was looking at a Renault.

The Renault salesman had two used cars—a Citroën *deux chevaux*, which looks like a plywood model for the VW beetle, and a barge of a Renault. Neither was what I wanted, but since I hadn't seen anything else, I tried them out.

As I got into the Renault, I reached for the seat belt. "Don't worry," the salesman said, "it's not *obligatoire*." Then he started discoursing on the recklessness of Togolese drivers, who are not as bad, however, as the Beninois, or, of course, the Nigerians.

In the *deux chevaux*, I knew better than to expect seat belts. The doors opened backward, the windows opened out, and the gear shift was on the dashboard. When I'd gotten it going more or less steadily on the sea road, the salesman directed the conversation to general topics.

"Where is your husband?" he asked.

"In the United States," I lied.

"What does he do?"

"He's a teacher, too."

"And your children?"

Children aren't really necessary, but they add to the verisimilitude, and he'd made it easy to have them. "They're home with my husband."

"And he lets you go off alone? For a whole year? He is very trusting."

Thursday, after three days, I'd made no progress. Philippe hadn't been able to contact his friend with the Peugeot, who has no phone and lives too far out of town for Philippe, who has no car, to go to see. Mac said the car his friend at the Honda dealership was working on wouldn't be a good buy. Simon's friends couldn't bring their cars by until Friday. And Marox had the same ads.

Today Marox had a new ad, for a 1982 Honda. My phone call was answered by the switchboard at the BIAO bank and the ad traced to a Mr. Douti, who said he'd bring the car right over (never mind that this was during business hours). Mr. Douti, a little man with a limp, was the picture of the embattled petty bureaucrat. He looked sewn into his dark pants and black velour jacket, gagged by his tie. I was disappointed to see that his car was a sleek white Quintet, a hatchback similar to the Accord. I'd pictured myself in something more basic, like a Civic.

"How much are you asking?" I asked.

"Do you like it?" he replied.

"It's more deluxe than I was looking for."

"Let's go for a ride," he said, "then we'll talk."

The car was comfortable and drove well. It had air conditioning, which after a week of traipsing around Lomé was beginning to seem more like a necessity than a luxury, and a tape player (with one speaker, the other had been stolen). Mr. Douti was asking 1.4 million CFA, or $3,500, and I figured he'd probably go down to 1.2 million. This was 200,000 CFA or $500 over what I had considered my top price. But the price I paid was really irrelevant if the car was worth it because I could recoup most of it when I sold the car in June. The real problem with this car was that it seemed ostentatious. I thought it would make me want to tell people,

"Look, I really have an old Volkswagen at home; I only bought this car because, believe it or not, it was the one that would cost me the least in the long run." If I wanted the car, I had to decide today because by Monday Mr. Douti would be on vacation—that is, home in an unnumbered house on an unnamed street without a phone—for a month.

"The difference," said Mac, "is between having a car and not having one. Once you have a car, it doesn't much matter what kind." He thought the car sounded like a great buy, and besides, he had another friend at the BIAO bank who must be Mr. Douti's boss, which fact should lower the price even more. So he called the bank and asked his friend to ask Mr. Douti to bring the car back in the afternoon for the embassy mechanic to look at.

At noon in Lomé, everything stops. Traffic clears off the streets, vendors doze in their stalls. Whatever business or anxiety you may have been immersed in goes on hold. I had a lunch date with Patrice's daughter. Patrice has been so helpful to me that when he told me earlier in the week that his daughter was "good in English" and wanted to go to college in the United States, I jumped at the chance to do something for him by inviting her to lunch and seeing if she really was a good candidate for American education. We took a taxi to the Mini-Brasserie, the only restaurant I know, and for the next hour, over chicken Provençale, I tried to draw out a shy, giggly seventeen-year-old, who, if she knew any English, was unwilling to speak it. What she really wanted was to escape to the Kung Fu matinée at the Opéra.

We walked back on the noon-quiet streets. After Angeline turned off, I found myself passing the Honda dealer. Out front was a white Civic with a for-sale sign. Just what I'd been looking for—and in the nick of time, before Simon's friends brought their cars over and Mr. Douti returned with his. The dealer was closed for lunch, but one of the men sitting on the curb told me he would bring the car to the Cultural Center at three.

The Civic showed up promptly, but I soon realized that it was in poor shape and not worth 800,000 CFA, which its sponsor assured me was the "last price" because it was being sold by *une blanche* like me. When I returned from the test drive, Mr. Douti had arrived. Mac and the embassy mechanic looked over his car and pronounced it good. I told Mac I'd buy it, and he undertook the bargaining, laying great stress on the fact that he could turn over the cash "right now." Mac put on a good show, but he had to bargain through an interpreter, and he settled at the figure I'd predicted;

I was pleased to realize I could have done as well myself. When the price was settled, he sent an embassy employee to the safe for cash, as I wrote out a check to the embassy and another employee began typing up an *attestation* for Mr. Douti to sign acknowledging that he had sold the car to me. Mr. Douti sat there looking stunned. I sympathized. "When things happen at the American embassy, they happen fast, don't they?" "Ah oui," he said, "les américains sont forts."

I was startled to see that Mr. Douti's birthdate on one of his papers was the same year as mine. I don't know whether I thought he was older or younger than I, but it never occurred to me that we might be age mates.

Only while waiting for the paperwork did I remember that Simon's friends would have arrived at the Cultural Center with their car. I dashed across the street, embarrassed to be late and to have to tell Simon's friends I'd already bought a car without seeing theirs. They were sitting patiently on the curb next to a white Honda Civic—the same one I'd just tried out, which also turned out to be the same car Mac's friend at the Honda dealer had mentioned. The other car Simon's friends had to offer they hadn't been able to bring over: Mr. Douti was showing it himself.

So I was destined to have one of these two Hondas. To sell a car, you tell all your friends, and if they find you a buyer, give them a cut. Simon's friends took their miss with good humor, and I promised to send any other prospective car buyers I encountered to them.

I drove Mr. Douti back to the bank. He went home in a taxi with $3,000 in his pocket and a plastic bag of the things he'd kept in the car. I soloed home in my new car, knuckles white on the steering wheel, eyes straining for potholes, pedestrians, and the inconspicuous traffic lights, right foot ready to hit the brake. The left turn across taxi traffic onto the Route d'Atakpamé felt like a blind leap into the abyss. In front of the taxi park, the cyclist in front of me wobbled and fell.

"We'll get you some insurance next week," Mac had said. "Until then, I wouldn't do much driving."

Tam-tam Funeral

☒ ☒ ☒ ☒ ☒ ☒

Saturday morning, while John the carpenter was here building shelves, Carol Luther-Hill dropped by on her way home from SGGG to ask if I'd like to go to a tam-tam society funeral in the afternoon.

Would I? I never expected traditional culture would be this accessible. Could I take my camera?

"Oh sure," said Carol, "bring your camera, they'll love it."

There are lots of tam-tam funeral societies in Lomé. They're supported by membership dues and perform funerals for their own members. They amount to a kind of funeral insurance as well as a social club. I already knew that funerals were a major social activity here. The obituaries are read every night on the radio, and Elise has complained that she never has time on weekends to do anything she'd like to do because she always has to go to a funeral. In this small country everybody is related in some way to nearly everybody else, and if you don't go to some distant cousin's or friend-of-a-friend's funeral, it's held against you in perpetuity. (When I saw Elise today and told her about going to the tam-tam funeral, she said she didn't know about *that* kind.) Carol and Kurt became honorary members of the tam-tam society after attending a few funerals with their Togolese neighbors. Now they feel obliged to go to a certain percentage of the society's funerals. They hadn't been to one in awhile, so they really had to go to this one, and—Carol didn't put it quite this way—having a wide-eyed newcomer along would make it more interesting for them.

Carol and Kurt and the neighbors picked me up a little after three, and we drove to a neighborhood not more than a mile from here, just off the Route d'Atakpamé. We were early, so Kurt inquired about the shop of a ritual sculptor he'd heard was in the neighborhood. The shop had a row of traditional stools painted on the front as a sign. The sculptor, a middle-

19

aged man missing most of his front teeth, seemed delighted to see us. He and his older children brought piece after piece out of the dark little storeroom into the courtyard to show us. Meanwhile, a woman squatting on the packed dirt washing dishes in an enamel basin glanced at us only occasionally, and two toddlers sat bare-bottomed on the ground putting bits of debris into their mouths. The carvings, in light unpainted wood, were human figures, some up to five feet high, with various startled expressions and animal features. Several had long ears, long tongues sticking out, and yard-long penises. They represent various spirits in voodoo, which is not a joke but a real and strong religion all along the coast from Lomé east into Benin. Kurt said this man was considered the best ritual sculptor in Togo and was pictured in a book on voodoo by a German anthropologist.

The sculptor walked back with us to the funeral site. The funeral seemed to be in part a celebration of the bold wax-print fabric that fills the markets and brightens the streets. The canopy over the site was a huge patchwork of *pagnes*, the six-yard lengths in which fabric is sold and, often, worn. We arrived with a free-form procession of women carrying chairs (the ubiquitous Danish modern and wooden kitchen chairs) on their heads. Groups of half a dozen or so wore dresses in the same pattern, and Carol told me that for special ceremonies the whole society dresses alike. The women's outfit, called a *complet*, is striking and becoming and no doubt hot—a fitted bodice with a variety of neck and sleeve detail including ruffles and tucks, a long, very straight skirt, and a *pagne* wrapped around the middle to hold the skirt and blouse together and carry a baby. It emphasizes the bust and buttocks to create an almost Edwardian silhouette. A street full of women, mincing and erect, creating flowing patterns of red-and-purple and green-and-gold against the lowering sun, looked more like a ceremonial procession than the transport of furniture. A boy of ten or so under a tree in front of a house across the street watched the procession while he gave himself a shower by dipping water out of a bucket.

The spectators sat outside the canopy in the shade of a building. We were given places of honor in the low Danish-modern chairs. On our left was what I took to be the bereaved family, two men in rich, handwoven *kente*-cloth *pagnes* with the end thrown over the shoulder like a toga, two women with gold chains draped over their hair and extravagant rose-and-purple make-up, all of them with fixed faces. In front of them was a little table on which sat one of the sculptor's carvings, a small seated mother and child, flanked by a bowl of plastic flowers and a covered dish containing membership booklets. The carving was painted realistically (though with pink skin). Whether because of the small size, or the relative realism, or the paint, it lacked the power of the unpainted pieces we'd seen in the sculptor's studio. The men on our right, wearing *kente* and dignified expressions, must have been the elders. Other spectators sat behind us on the higher kitchen chairs. I was envying their view when one of the men in charge came over and told me to feel free to walk around and take any pictures I wanted.

The performers filled four rows of benches set in a square under the canopy. They faced each other to make two aisles. On one side of the square were the musicians, who played the tam-tams and shook rattles made from calabashes covered with nets laced with cowries. In the center of the square, a couple of men led the singing and dancing and a cassette player provided more music. The dancing started slowly and gradually increased in intensity. The dancers swayed back and forth at their seats and filed down the aisles between the rows. The leaders shook horsetails and sang to various people in the audience including the bereaved family, the elders, the Luther-Hills, and me. As the rhythm quickened, a clown appeared, a short plump woman with bare shoulders, feathers tucked into a turban, and sunglasses with one lens missing, carrying her own horsetail and an empty flashlight case. She danced on the benches, tickled people with her horsetail, hammed for the camera, flirted with the elders. Eventually one of the elders stood up and pressed a coin to her forehead, where it stuck in the sweat. Periodically a couple of women came over to the bereaved family to repowder the women's impassive faces and reperfume their armpits. There was nothing funereal about the atmosphere. I got the impression that the purpose of the ceremony was to cheer up the bereaved, who, however, did not respond.

At first, despite the invitation, I was diffident about taking photographs, especially direct portraits of the more ceremonious-looking individuals. I focused on the colorful mass of dancers, children hanging on the fringes, a couple of girls of about four and six dressed like their mother and imitating her movements, a man in a wraparound *pagne* and a T-shirt that said "J'aime le Togo" with a heart dotting the *i*. When I'd taken a couple of shots of some boys carrying vegetable oil—tin buckets strung on ropes over their foreheads, one of the elders I'd been shy of got up in exasperation and gestured that I better take a picture of him before I used up my film on riffraff. I pulled another roll of film out of my pocket to reassure him, then turned my lens on him. He settled back, adjusted his cloth and his expression, and held out his wrist to show off his Eyadéma watch. This watch has a striped strap in red, green, and yellow, the colors of the Togolese flag, and a black face on which every thirty seconds appears the portrait of the president, Gnassingbé Eyadéma. I smiled my thanks, and he acknowledged me with the faintest flicker of his eyelids.

As the sun dropped low and the dancing reached a climax, the women who had been attending to the toilette of the bereaved circulated through the audience. First, they showered us with confetti. Then, one patted each face with a towel, while the other poured perfume into our hands for us to splash on our faces. Finally, they marked our left forearms with two fingers dipped in a white paste of, I think, powder and perfume. I kept trying to protect the camera from these unforeseen blessings without appearing ungrateful.

Then the dancers began to break from their rows and dance on their own. They thrust their shoulder blades, elbows, and buttocks back, chests and knees forward, and moved like strutting, pecking chickens. The sculptor and a toothless man in a faded wax-print toga and checked wool driving cap competed, laughing, to see who could squat lower. The members of the bereaved family allowed themselves to be pulled up and made dancing gestures, still without a flicker of expression. An old woman pulled me up and laughed at my efforts to dance. Next time, she says, she'll teach me.

On the way home in the car, I asked the Luther-Hills' neighbor about what we'd seen—who had died, how long since, what the songs were about, what the carving of the mother and child signified, what the two-fingered mark meant. But I didn't learn much. The person had died "some time ago." The carving was the society's symbol. I don't think he was deliberately withholding information, because the people at the funeral were so open. Maybe the problem was that neither of us was used to talking about these things in French. Maybe he wasn't used to thinking about the separate parts of a traditional ceremony as having meaning. Kurt said later that this had been the ceremony to close the one-year period of mourning and I'd been right that its thrust was to cheer up the bereaved.

When I cleaned up to go to a party at Kay's afterward, I was careful not to wash off the two-fingered white mark. But at the party either no one noticed it or everyone was too polite to say anything.

Martin/Mahouna

✉ ✉ ✉ ✉ ✉ ✉

I've settled the question of hours and pay with Martin. He'll come five mornings a week and I'll pay him 20,000 CFA a month. To reach this figure, we started from the embassy scale, which pays 20,000 to a full-time houseboy (working sixty hours a week) and adjusted it for the fact that Flint paid him more per hour for fewer hours and that it will be hard for him to find another half-time job since the pay for full-time is so low. Then there was the question of social security, for which the employer is supposed to pay 18.2 percent and the employee 1.8 percent of salary. But Martin has never registered with social security and doesn't want any money he's earned to go there because he's sure he'll never see it again. Mac Macdowell hinted that he expects me to follow the rules, but I don't know whether social security here really protects a worker or not. And if I insist on going by the rules for the one year I'm here, Martin will be registered and have to pay from now on. So instead I'm paying him for the two summer months before the next Fulbrighter arrives. If full-time pay for a half-time job seems generous, consider that it's still only $50 a month. If that seems stingy, consider that the minimum wage is 500 francs or $1.25 for a ten-hour day.

So salary is settled, but now there's a new problem: what to call him. Before I left, my friend Sylvia gave me two rules for getting along with domestic employees: Always address them as *vous* and get a receipt for their pay, because when she left Cameroun her long-time houseboy accused her of not paying him. The receipt seemed like a good idea, especially as my lodging expenses are income tax deductible, so I bought a receipt book and the first time I paid Martin I asked him to fill one out and sign it. He stiffened and didn't relax until I explained income tax deductions and record keeping. When I looked at his signature, though, I was puzzled. It didn't correspond to either "Martin" or his family name. He said it represented his "real" name, Mahouna, which means "God-given."

"If Mahouna is your real name," I said, "would you like me to call you that?"

"I don't care," he said.

"You must care," I said, "it's your *name*."

"It's up to you," he said.

"It's not up to me," I said, "it's *your* name."

"I don't care," he said.

It would be easier to go on calling him "Martin," since I'm already used to it and that's what the other Europeans in the *cité* call him. (They know him because he delivers beer and soda by the case and provides a utility bill–paying service; he collects bills and money and stands in line downtown to pay.) But having introduced the idea of respecting his "real" name, I didn't feel I could go back to the European name that is "easier" for Europeans unless he asked me to. So I'm trying to get used to calling him "Mahouna," while not at all sure he appreciates it.

As for *vousvoyer*ing the help, Mahouna has *tutoyé*ed me from the beginning. So have the carpenter, the plumber, and the job seekers. The only Togolese I've heard use *vous* are the professional staff at the embassy— Patrice and Simon Amégavie, for example. Simon sounds just like a high-school French textbook. Whenever he sees me in the Cultural Center he says, "Bonjour, mademoiselle. Comment allez-vous? Vous allez bien?" Most domestic workers do seem to call their employers, Europeans anyway, "madame" or "monsieur," but not Mahouna. At first, I was just "*tu*"; then "Mademoiselle Zoozahn"; now I'm "Zoozahn."

The problem of naming extends to the inanimate things we have to talk about. Mahouna wants me to write out a schedule of what he should do every day. In the first place, I don't know all the things that will need to be done, or how often the floor needs to be washed; in the second place, I don't care whether he wipes the grit off the window louvers on Tuesday or Thursday. He knows a lot more about taking care of this apartment than I do. I want to say, just keep up with things and make sure there's enough water boiled and I'll be satisfied. But he wants to be covered.

Beyond all that, though, I don't have the vocabulary to make up a schedule. What do you call "stove," "oven," "kitchen counter," the built-in cabinets in the living room? Pascal and Proust didn't deal with these things, and the little paperback French-English dictionary I brought offers nothing or too many choices in each instance. Mahouna doesn't know either. His French is excellent, but as academic as mine. He seems to have cleaned these things without naming them. So we've agreed on terms, but they'd probably surprise any French housewife.

Mahouna did tell me that the utility room off the kitchen is called *la buanderie*, which is sometimes corrupted to *la boyerie* because that's where *le boy* spends much of his time. And if *le boy* is a woman, he says, the French may call her *la boyesse*.

I said I didn't like the term *boy*, and he replied with heat that he didn't either. I asked what was a better alternative. He said the official term for domestic employees is *gens de maison*, but that's a plural that has no singular. Then there's *domestique*. That sounds okay in French, but in English *domestic* sounds either incomplete, an adjective without a noun, or feminine. You could say *helper*, but no one would guess what you were talking about. I've heard that an eccentric Englishman here calls his employee a *steward*, which is pretty neutral and accurate, but an American can't get away with a Briticism without sounding affected. Actually, Mahouna has some characteristics of the classic British butler—proprietariness, dignity, discretion; but then no butler swabs down the floor with wet rags. Maybe I'll try *housekeeper*, which sounds odd (and again, feminine) but is at least accurate and recognizable.

So I have a housekeeper named Mahouna, when anyone I would mention him to understands me to have a houseboy named Martin.

Expats

Expatriate social life is frenetic. I feel like a cross between Mrs. Ramsay and Isabel Archer. Since classes haven't started yet, I have nothing to do but manage the house and keep social engagements, and it feels like a full-time job.

The first Sunday I was here, for example, I went to the beach with Kay. Back at her house, after too much midday sun, we were barely out of the shower (bliss!) when people started dropping in. First Vera and Philippe Ekoué, who met Kay through the English language classes at the Cultural Center, where Vera, who is Ghanaian, has been a teacher and Philippe, Togolese, a student. Vera is a sort of semi-expatriate. She grew up in a diplomatic family and went to high school in England. As an Ewe, she is at home in this part of Togo (the Ghana-Togo border divides the Ewe people), but as an English speaker and English-educated professional she feels not only like a foreigner but like one from a more developed country. Compared to the military hospital in Accra, where she trained as a nurse-midwife, she considers Lomé the medical boondocks. Philippe, who grew up in Lomé and recently started working for ECOWAS (Economic Community of West African States), is just getting acquainted with the international perspective Vera takes for granted. He seems to be feeling his way in a new world.

Kay was trying to get the BBC on the shortwave to hear a report on the KAL plane that had just been shot down over the Soviet Union when her neighbor, an embassy secretary about to leave Togo, came over to invite us to her house to see her Malian mud cloth hangings before she packed them. Kay wouldn't let us go until she'd served a blender full of commissary frozen orange juice. At the neighbor's, another Cultural Center English teacher dropped in, and we all stayed for tea and cake.

When Kay took me home, exhausted, about ten, as we were getting out of the car in the driveway a yellow Golf pulled up and an Englishwoman named Callie Lloyd and a Togolese named René got out and introduced themselves. I didn't catch René's last name, and it took me a minute to realize he wasn't Callie's husband (who is Trevor). They knew all about me in advance though and had been waiting for me to turn up. Callie tried to recruit me for the play she intends to direct and René wanted to know if I played tennis.

This past Friday I went to dinner at the Lloyds'. They live in one of the smaller "villas" in the *cité*, a three-bedroom house with a lovely garden and—startling to see—grass. Until this year they taught at the American School, but Trevor was fired and Callie quit and now they are starting a school of their own they call "The British School of Lomé," though it has no official British status, in the building in the *cité* that was planned as a school and is labeled "Ecole." They're thus in mutually contemptuous competition with my friends at the American School. Trevor is the headmaster, Callie the assistant head (though she is the one who negotiates with the Togolese bureaucracy because Trevor doesn't speak French). The occasion for the dinner was to welcome the one other teacher. René was there, too.

Callie and Trevor seem blindly British. A week or so ago, I called on Callie in the afternoon. While we were having tea, a German woman with hesitant English came to enroll her son in the school. Callie explained the dress code. After a bit they'll have a proper uniform, but in the meantime, boys are to wear long pants, no shorts, and a short-sleeved shirt, not a T-shirt, "you know, a proper shirt." The German woman didn't seem to find this description clear.

Friday when we arrived, Callie was in the midst of instructing her new houseboy to change the napkins; he'd actually put out *tea* napkins for a dinner party. This led right into the topic that I've already found a dinner party staple, servants. Callie wouldn't want Martin (that is, Mahouna) to work for her because "he doesn't think of himself as a houseboy."

And yet, both Callie and Trevor are young, under thirty I'd guess, and they told stories of their adventurous youth, hitchhiking around the United States, squatting in empty buildings in Amsterdam. They drove to Africa overland from England in a Land Rover still sitting in their driveway, were robbed while camping on the beach in Benin, and settled in Togo because they ran out of money. The stories of their travels don't go with the picture they present of complacent colonials.

Merle, the new teacher, is about fifty, a bleached blonde with leathery skin and a dramatic manner. She's had a career as a sort of international governess, preparing pupils in various parts of the world for British exams. She kept comparing the novice houseboy to the well-trained stewards she was accustomed to in Sierra Leone.

When she heard that Mahouna worked for me only in the mornings, she said she'd employ him in the afternoons. So intimate a connection with Merle as a shared housekeeper does not appeal to me. And I'd rather not subject Mahouna to someone who seems to share Callie's view of houseboys. But an afternoon job in the same neighborhood is exactly what he wants. It's probably all one to him whether he adjusts to a Briton who knows what she wants or an American who doesn't. And the last thing he needs is protection from more income. So I'll have to tell him about Merle's offer and look forward to conversation initiatives at the pool or parties not just about servants but about Mahouna.

Through this whole colonial conversation, René managed to smile sympathetically at the houseboy when he removed the underdone fish and agree with Callie that you can't have good things because houseboys will break them. René's interesting. He's about Callie and Trevor's age but has the polish of someone older. He works for a labor education center sponsored by the AFL-CIO; speaks perfect English, as well as French, Ewe, Mina, Fon, and some German; and seems to know everyone of any consequence in Lomé. He talked about a photographic project he's doing on the Tamberma, a group of hunter-gatherers in northern Togo largely untouched by colonialism and modernization. He says he's learned some of their language and made the contacts to gain access to the society. He seems to be committed to Togo, yet more comfortable with Europeans.

And yet not completely comfortable. When Callie started planning "a real Christmas lunch with suet pudding" to be held at the school, he told a story of the miserable way he spent last Christmas. He would have gone to celebrate Christmas in his village near Kpalimé, but instead he accepted an invitation to go somewhere with some American friends, and they never showed up. It seemed an oddly ingenuous story, maybe a tribute to Callie and Trevor that they wouldn't treat him like that or a plea to me not to. Somehow we discovered that we have the same birthday, and he instantly started planning a joint party.

Saturday night I went to a birthday party organized by some American PVO (private voluntary organization) workers. They'd each invited people they knew with the result that there was a mix of Americans, Canadians,

Germans, and French from an assortment of development agencies. The apartment where the party was held was big and empty except for a stereo. Everybody brought a foam chair cushion to sit on. Those who had been to the U.S. recently brought the latest music. The dancers had one end of the room, and the talkers sprawled on the cushions at the other end, shouting over the music. There was beer and cheese curls and sour-cream onion dip and the familiar clutter of empty potato-chip bags in the kitchen. It was loud and hot, and I realized all of a sudden what made it so refreshing: no houseboys. Nobody was "madame" or "monsieur." But there were no Togolese guests either.

TUESDAY, SEPTEMBER 20

Home Improvement

✉ ✉ ✉ ✉ ✉ ✉ ✉

I've become an habituée of the hardware departments of SGGG. I join the plumbers and electricians maneuvering for attention from indifferent clerks on the other side of the counter. Mary Kingsley was the "first white woman" on the banks of the Ogowé; I could be the first woman, period, in the hardware departments of SGGG.

My first expedition was a great success. The plumbing supply clerk understood *bouchon d'évier* to mean sink stopper and *rondelles* to mean washers. The pocket dictionary was working. At the electrical counter, I could point to the swing-arm desk lamp I wanted. At the last minute I remembered to ask for a bulb for the lamp.

When I plugged the lamp into the electrical outlet behind the desk, however, nothing happened. The nearest outlet that works is beside the bed on the opposite wall. The next day I went back to SGGG for an extension cord. When I asked for a *fil d'extension*, the clerk looked blank. I tried to think of another way to say "extension cord" but couldn't. Finally I resorted to dramatic explanation: "J'ai une lampe ici," I said, pointing to the counter, "mais le"—here I wanted to say that the electrical outlet was far away, but I suddenly realized I didn't know the term for electrical outlet, so I improvised with "la source d'électricité," which must have sounded quaint, because *source* means "spring." When the clerk eventually produced an extension cord, the label said *rallonge*.

Since the cord has to pass in front of the closet doors and the door to the porch, I wanted insulated staples to tack it down to the carpet. The dictionary translated "staple" as *clou à deux points* and "insulated" as *isolé*, but "clous à deux points isolés" meant nothing to the clerk. I said I wanted to "attacher la rallonge au plancher." Perhaps to get rid of me, he said he had nothing like that, I should try UAC downtown on the rue de Commerce. At UAC, three clerks listened with sympathy to my explanation about attaching an extension cord to the floor, but the best they could come up with was masonry nails. They suggested I try Batimat a few blocks away.

I'd walked a couple of blocks when I heard someone calling, "Madame, madame." In this part of town, "madame, madame" is the cry of beggars, money changers, and curio vendors, so I hoped I wasn't the one addressed and walked on. Soon a plump young man in a white shirt and tie came puffing up behind me. "I called to you, but you didn't hear me," he panted. It was the son of the owner of UAC; he said he knew what I wanted and he could explain it to the personnel in Batimat.

When we arrived, he spoke to the clerk, who led us to—those gizmos, I've forgotten their name, that hold a screw in a hollow wall. The UAC owner's son looked crushed when I said, no, that wasn't what I wanted. But Batimat itself was a find: Everything is displayed, you can look for what you want. I combed the aisles and eventually found what people here use to keep electrical cords in place. It's a three-quarter-inch nail with a plastic loop. No wonder they didn't understand my description of insulated staples. A nail won't work on my bedroom floor, which is cement under the carpet. Now what I need is duct tape. I wonder what that's called—or if it exists in a tropical country.

Meanwhile, Elise has helped me with decor. Yesterday she came to my house for lunch and afterward took me to a basket market and a nursery. The basket market is alongside a narrow, muddy, potholed road behind GoyiScore, the other French supermarket. I was looking for big straw mats to hang over the water stains on the living room wall. I had just about bought one with Elise's help, as the women selling them didn't speak French, when Elise decided to compare the price at the stall across the street. This woman, it turned out, had a better mat at a lower price. The first vendor flew into a rage. What was Elise doing taking the part of a *yovo* against her own people? Who did she think she was, driving up in a big car (she pointed to the mud-splashed Honda parked awkwardly up the road) and cheating her own people on the *yovo*'s behalf? If it weren't for her, the *yovo* would have paid much more. The woman didn't refuse to sell me the smaller things I'd picked out from her display, but I still felt subdued as we picked our way around the mudholes back to the car.

As we turned a corner on our way to the nursery, a policeman standing beside the road started waving his arms and shouting.

"You'd better stop," said Elise.

The policeman said something I didn't understand, and Elise told me he claimed I had turned without using the directional signal.

Here I realized it was my turn to take charge. "Oh, monsieur," I said, in my most ingratiating manner, "I am sorry, but I am new in Lomé and don't know my way around, and madame here was directing me, and I didn't know she wanted me to turn here until the last minute."

He looked back and forth between us; he seemed surprised. Was it that I had stood up to him? The first thing I heard when I bought the car was to be super careful as Europeans are held responsible for any mishap or infraction. Or was it that he saw a European and a Togolese in a companionable relationship, with the European taking direction from the Togolese? The irony of that would be that I was really doing a gracious-lady act by pointing to the relationship and expecting it to cover for an infraction. In any case, he said, "Well, I'll let it go this time. But be careful."

"You're lucky," said Elise. "Usually they fine you, and you have to pay on the spot. This is a bad time, just before school opens. The policemen don't get paid much, and they need extra money for school fees and supplies. They'll stop you whenever they think they can get away with it. The same thing happens around Christmas and Easter."

At the nursery, I bought a big flat pot of cheerful pink flowers to put by the apartment entrance. Then I was glad enough to take Elise home and call it a day.

Chez Mahouna
✉ ✉ ✉ ✉ ✉

Mahouna is proud of the car. When I brought it home, he said, now I will come at seven every morning to wash the car before you go out. Oh no, I replied, the car doesn't need to be washed every day. And eight o'clock, I was thinking, is early enough to be intruded upon. We compromised on seven-thirty.

Then he said, now that you have the car, you can come to my house for dinner.

A dinner invitation from the *domestique?* This was a contingency Sylvia wouldn't have dreamed of. Did it mean that Mahouna was taking my effort to establish a friendly employer-employee relationship seriously? Or that he was taking it too far?

I went last night. Mahouna came on foot to get me about seven o'clock. I had never seen him before in anything but his work clothes, dark pants and a white shirt. I didn't even realize they were his work clothes. Now he was wearing shorts so short they barely showed under his dashiki, a porkpie hat, and a big grin. It was like being picked up for a date.

He had to guide me to his house because there was no way to explain how to get there. We went through the university to a *quartier* of unpaved streets behind it. "Comme ci, comme ça," Mahouna kept saying by way of telling me to turn left and right. In the dark, with no street names and no obvious landmarks, I quickly lost all sense of direction. At first we snaked around and slogged through thick red puddles. The farther we got from the university, the more seriously the streets were eroded. They became a network of rocky chasms. At each intersection, I had to look ahead and figure out how to get through. "Doucement, doucement," Mahouna coached, "slowly, slowly." Chickens strolled out of the way and children ran alongside. The sleek white car, proudly polished by Mahouna in the morning, seemed more and more out of place.

As soon as we pulled up children poured out of the house, a compound with a central courtyard surrounded by rooms. More reticent adults waited inside the courtyard. As Mahouna showed off me and the car, I realized I should have brought my camera and something for the children. I hadn't been thinking of this evening as an occasion for reciprocal cultural display.

Mahouna is the aristocrat of the compound. Most of the rooms are occupied by an entire family; he has his all to himself. He is the one who divides up the electric bill and collects from each family. This is a good deal for him, he pointed out, because each household pays according to the number of electrical appliances they have, with no distinction between a light bulb and a refrigerator. Some of the families, I could see, had a television, but Mahouna was the only one with a refrigerator, and as he said, "Ça consume." The refrigerator itself is a money-maker because it enables him to sell ice and cold drinks to his neighbors. With the profit he makes on this business, he lends money by the month.

His room was perhaps ten feet by twelve. To the left of the door, a bed was curtained off. On the far wall stood the refrigerator and cases of soda. On the wall to the right was a small bookcase with a few books and a radio. Above it, a *National Geographic* map of Africa, given him by an earlier Fulbrighter. The table, in front of the door, was neatly set with a cloth, a jar of frangipani and bougainvillea flowers, and two places. The plates were turned upside down, and a Bière Bénin coaster covered each glass to keep out dust and bugs.

Mahouna switched on the radio, a bit loud to talk over, and opened the refrigerator. What would I like to drink? The expansive host had everything. I took advantage of the opportunity to try *sodabi*, the liquor distilled from palm wine (rather like gin). I admired the arrangements. One of the books was Ferdinand Oyono's *Une vie de boy* (translated as *Boy* or *Houseboy*), a story of the ironies and injustices of the mistress-servant rela- tion. I was surprised that he had read a novel; he was surprised that I'd read one about his life. He also showed me notebooks from the night courses in economics he has been taking at the university for the last ten years. He volunteered that he hasn't passed a course yet. This year, he says, he is going to take law instead.

When we'd completed the tour of the room, we sat down and Ma- houna summoned his twelve-year-old cousin Gabriel to serve the meal. Gabriel lives with Mahouna (sleeps on the floor) so he can go to school, serves as houseboy and cook, and minds the beverage business while Mahouna is at work. Mahouna directed him to serve just as Clarence does at Kay's. We had grilled chicken and *djencoumé*, a stiff cornmeal mush cooked in chicken broth with bits of tomato and hot pepper (omitted this time for my benefit). The neighborhood children hung in the doorway watching the spectacle until Mahouna told Gabriel to give them some bread and send them away.

With dinner, Mahouna wanted me to drink "wine." I was inclined to prefer beer, as wine is imported and relatively expensive. But he insisted. This wine was local. What was it made from? Grapes. Grapes? I hadn't seen any grapevines in Togo. Where do the grapes grow? On the grape tree.

It turns out that the grape tree is a common one I've noticed in the *cité* with pinkish berries from which people make a rough wine. I'd never heard of this wine before, and neither has any of the Americans I asked in the Cultural Center today. Drinking it gave me a fleeting sensation of slipping into a world I hadn't suspected existed, where words we take for granted have different meanings and things we think can't be done are.

Mahouna kept pressing drinks on me, touching the loaded refrigerator that made him a businessman instead of a servant. I kept declining because I knew what a neighborhood event a trip to the latrine (if there was one) would be. So our respective efforts to preserve our dignity clashed.

When we left, the neighbors came out again to say good-bye, and I promised to return with my camera. As I renegotiated the crisscrossing chasms, Mahouna said he had brought me to his house because he knew I was a stranger, far from my people, and if I ever needed help he wanted me to know where to find him. I know he was sincere; he feels he's a stranger in Lomé, too, with no family but Gabriel. At the same time, I know he also wanted his neighbors to see him on social terms with a white woman in a fine car and for me to see that he had a radio, a map, and a servant and knew how to set a table and be a host.

When we reached paved roads and I knew where I was, I urged Mahouna to start back. I thought he was being too protective and I didn't want to lengthen his walk. But he stayed till we got to the main road so he could get a taxi back. This morning he washed the evidence of the night's expedition off the car.

Village Visit

✉ ✉ ✉ ✉

Yesterday I got out of Lomé. Friday afternoon the Lloyds' friend René found me at the pool when he arrived to play tennis and asked me to go dancing that evening. We sampled two nightclubs, each international in its own way—L'Abreuvoir, where we watched the dance of African prostitutes and expatriate men, and Le Chess, the strobe-lit *boîte* in the international-class Hôtel du Deux Février, where we danced to mostly European music with a mixed African and European crowd. On the way home, René suggested we go to Tabligbo on Saturday to visit a Peace Corps friend of his. Tabligbo has a *cité* like Lomé's with a swimming pool and tennis courts; I could swim while René and Fritz played tennis.

The drive was glorious. The coast road east to Aného near the Benin border goes through a postcard paradise of coconut groves and fishing villages. Near Lomé, a lone Portuguese colonial house stands abandoned in a field. A hand-painted sign with a picture of a mermaid and the information "Féticheur" points down a grassy path. Farther on we watched villagers in two lines haul a fish-laden blue net onto the beach. We stopped for a *limonade* at the hotel in Aného, where you sit on the terrace and look across the lagoon to the old Portuguese colonial part of town, thoroughly romantic from that distance. (Even the casual tourist can see shadows on paradise, though. A wide yellow-green stain spreads out into the ocean from the phosphate plant at Kpémé, Togo's main industry, and the erosion from the ocean is so bad that in places the edge of the road has been eaten away.)

From Aného we turned north into grassland. Here, at the approach of the car, the people walking along the road jumped far off into the tall grass and waved. I asked René why people waved. As fellow travelers on a little-used path? Or the way, as kids, we used to wave to trains hoping to be recognized by people in a different world? He said, not very helpfully, that they were just being friendly.

36

Near Vogan, René suddenly remarked, as though he'd just thought of it, that he had a cousin who lived in a village somewhere nearby. She had come to Lomé asking for money, and he would like to see how she lived. Would I mind detouring to try to find her? As if I'd turn down the chance to visit a village.

René didn't know what village she lived in, or her married name, only that her husband was a schoolteacher. The postmaster in Vogan, who was just closing up for the afternoon, pondered and asked what village she had been born in. René named the village, near Kpalimé, on the other side of the country, and the postmaster said, ah yes, he had heard that the school-master in such-and-such village was married to a woman from the village René named; he knew who could take us there. He got into the car and directed us to a house nearby. A man came out and said, "Wé zonlo," which is Mina for "welcome." René had been teaching me Mina greetings, so I knew enough to reply with him, "Yo lo." The postmaster explained what we wanted to the man, who called his teenage daughter and explained to her; she went back inside and changed into a handsome *complet*, then got into the car to direct us to the village. It seemed a long way, up a rocky track from Vogan, then through fields and bush. All along the way, people were walking to and from the Vogan market.

We parked under a tree beside the school, an open pavillion with a shoulder-high concrete-block wall, a thatched roof, and rows of benches inside. Off at the edge of the clearing was an outhouse with three doors—marked "Garçons," "Filles," and "Maîtres."

René's cousin came out of the little mud-brick house with a baby on her hip and a three-year-old and a five-year-old clutching her *pagne*. Her husband and two older children had gone to Aného for the day. While she and René talked, I looked around the yard. The kitchen was a mud-walled cylinder with a couple of feet of space between the top of the wall and the thatched roof. The utensils—clay pots, several enamel basins, an alumi-num tea kettle—sat on top of the wall beneath the thatch. A child's wooden scooter and some broken pottery lay on the ground. Two chickens pecked about. Off in a corner of the yard was the chicken-house, a beehive dome of woven sticks.

When René announced that we'd like to take pictures, his cousin changed from her *pagne* (wrapped under the arms as at-home wear) to a dress. We took pictures of everybody, including our guide, and the guide took one of all the rest of us with both René's camera and mine. Then the cousin took us on a tour of the village. Her husband's mentor, she said, would be very hurt if she didn't take us to meet him. "Dropping in" on René's cousin began to take on the character of a state visit.

We walked past houses, small garden patches, and a bare area where the children played soccer, to fields at the edge of the village, where corn and cassava were growing. A very tall old woman stood straight-legged, bent from the hips, washing clothes in a basin on the ground. When we passed, she straightened up and stood proudly, her flat breasts hanging to her waist, to have her picture taken. We collected children all along the way. When we took a group picture of them, they laughed and mugged and held their fingers up in a V-sign. One hopped along leaning on a stick; many had the bulbous navel of an umbilical hernia; most, the bloated belly of malnutrition. We met the chief at the shrine to the kola nut tree. He and a dozen other people were sitting on and around the steps of a white stucco house that had been built around the tree. Pictures of animals—a lion, a lizard, a snake—had been painted on the walls. As we approached, a woman who had been sitting there topless hoisted her *pagne* up from her waist to cover her breasts. The chief offered us kola nuts, which I tried and René knew enough to decline: bitter.

The cousin's husband's mentor, sitting with another group in the shade of a house, welcomed us extravagantly. I tried out my Mina greetings, then left the conversation to René, as no one there but his cousin spoke French. When a calabash of water was passed, presenting the eternal dilemma between health and manners, René told me quietly that I could simply dribble a little on the ground for the ancestors without drinking any. Then the mentor sent a child for soft drinks and invited us into his house.

The room was hot and dim. We sat facing each other on two beds—the mentor and the cousin and her baby on one; René, our guide, and I on the other—with a patch of light from the open doorway between us. It's clearly impossible to make a brief call on a personage in a village. He has to send out for drinks; you have to wait till they come and stay to drink them. So we had plenty of time for a conversation in which everything was said in two languages. René interpreted for me, using French rather than English to include his cousin. He prompted the mentor to tell about his relationship with the cousin's husband. I asked him about an old photograph of, it turned out, his grandfather, an old man draped in *kente* and leaning on a stick, who had been a chief. René's cousin stayed in the background as though she weren't there herself, only standing in for her husband. Our guide sat quiet and interested, perfectly poised through a long afternoon of other people's relatives.

When the messenger returned with four half-liter bottles of bubble gum–flavored soda, the mentor opened them all at once with a flourish. He took five glasses out of a little cupboard between the beds; the cousin took them outside to wash, then wiped each one carefully with a clean towel. After the first glassful, we were urged to accept more, but fortunately there were children willing to empty the bottles, and René could use me and the long drive we had ahead of us and the promise of a longer visit another time as reasons to leave after what would have been otherwise a rudely short visit of only three hours. He said after we'd dropped off our guide and gone on toward Tabligbo that he would never let people in a village like that know he was coming because they'd prepare a feast they couldn't afford.

When we got to Tabligbo after four, Fritz had just returned from a day in Aného, so we wouldn't have found him if we'd arrived as planned. But I'm not sure that René hadn't planned on going to the village from the beginning. He hadn't brought his tennis racket.

We drove back to Lomé through Tsévié, mostly in the dark (not recommended), and had a late dinner at Keur Rama, a restaurant on the Boulevard Circulaire with a bistro atmosphere and a pan-African menu. The owner is a Togolese woman who lived for some time in Senegal; the name means "Rama's Place" in Wolof. We were both exhausted and ravenous, having had nothing but soda and peanuts since breakfast. I was desperate for the washroom after a hot afternoon of walking around the dusty village. René was depressed about his cousin's circumstances. Her husband has only a junior-high education, all that's required to teach primary school, and doesn't make much money. She has five children already, and he doubts that she's able to keep from having more. She grew up used to better, he said. René ordered *gari* (made from cassava) with agouti (bush rat) in spinach sauce. I was too tired and hungry to venture far from the familiar, so I had rice with chicken in peanut sauce.

Friday afternoon before René appeared at the pool, I felt I was on my own for the first time. The people who were going to help me get settled or invite me somewhere because I was new had done so; I was facing a weekend alone and thinking about how I was going to get to know Togo beyond the *cité* and the American Cultural Center. Now I seem to have a regular escort. René is talking about traveling all over Togo as though we'll go together. This seems a hasty commitment on his part. If he did indeed plan the "detour" to the village, I wonder if he regarded it as a test.

I could hardly ask for a more ideal travel companion. He knows Togo and Americans, knew for example just what I needed to know when the water was passed in the village. Knows what to say in every situation and any language necessary to say it in. Has an outsider's curiosity as well as insider's familiarity. Is charming and considerate. He just seems so far ahead of me.

In fact, I'm just remembering something else he said about visiting the village again. He said we'd go back sometime, announced, take food for a feast, and stay overnight. I thought, wouldn't this be tantamount to announcing our engagement? But for some reason I didn't say anything. Didn't want to believe it perhaps, or was too busy keeping my balance to deal with that.

Bypass Plumbing
⊠ ⊠ ⊠ ⊠ ⊠ ⊠

Last week the phone was connected. I had filled out the papers and paid the fees two weeks before, and there was a phone in the apartment when I arrived, but getting it connected was a week's project. I would drive down to the embassy and call on Patrice, who would telephone his friend at the PTT, who would say, "The phone will be connected tomorrow." "Tomorrow" nothing would happen. After this had been repeated a few times, Patrice's friend, a manager, said he would come out and connect it himself. Patrice had me drive him to the PTT so he could show me where to find his friend. The next day I picked up the friend, brought him here to work on the phone, and returned him to the PTT. The day after that, I drove down to the embassy to ask Patrice to call and find out why the phone still didn't work. It's no wonder more people don't have phones; getting one takes not only a lot of money but also connections and a car. I still don't have a phone book, for which I'll have to apply at another office in the PTT.

Success with the phone made me think that maybe I didn't have to live with the feeble water pressure. So last Thursday, Mahouna and I went to the Régie des Eaux to inquire. To my surprise, the official we talked to said, "You're right, it shouldn't be like that, we'll send somebody out tomorrow."

Nothing happened Friday, but this morning, a truck full of workers arrived. The man in charge decided the old iron pipe from the main to the apartment was clogged, left five workers to dig up my driveway and replace the pipe with plastic, and drove off with the rest of his crew. The five, who all appeared to be teenagers, worked all day. They had to break up the cement in the driveway and dig a trench about five feet deep and thirty feet long in the hard clay underneath to take out the pipe. There was a clear division of labor. Two of them took turns wielding the pickax, two others laid the new pipe, the one in charge performed the dramatic actions, like turning the water back on.

It was a real neighborhood event. I took photographs at each stage, and before long the plumbers started calling me before they did anything new. When they wanted to seal a joint in the pipe, they gathered some palm fronds, asked me for a match, and made a little fire in the carport. The old men who hang out at the Conciergérie showed up to offer advice. Mathilde, the maid to my mystery neighbor two doors down, assured me that, yes, the Régie was very responsible, as opposed to the electric authority, which will turn off your electricity even if you have paid your bill.

I took Cokes out to the workers every so often, and when they were still here at noon, Mahouna went out on his bicycle to buy more bread so I could give them bread and cheese. They could have gotten a real meal from the women who sell food under the trees behind the swimming pool, but the head plumber said they didn't want to stop work until they'd finished. And they probably weren't carrying any money. The bathing trunks they wore and the shirts they tossed in a heap on the ground didn't have pockets.

About five thirty, the job seemed to be done. The head plumber joined the last joint and turned the water on, and I went into the house to test the faucets.

Nothing. Not even a drizzle.

The Greek chorus from the Conciergérie shook their heads. Nothing to be done, because the plumbing is the Régie's responsibility only up to the house. Inside the house, it's the responsibility of the Caisse (the social security administration, which administers the *cité*), with which one communicates via the Conciergérie, which was by now closed for the day. And anyway, it would take at least a week to get the Caisse to do anything. No water for a week, they assured me.

Not to worry, said the head plumber, he'd take care of me. He knew what was wrong, but he needed some parts to fix it. He would treat me like his mother, and I would treat him like my son. When he saw that I was a bit taken aback by this relationship, he revised it: If I would take him to buy the parts, and pay for them, and "treat him like my little brother," I could have water tonight.

So, leaving the others sitting in the carport, we drove off to SGGG. SGGG didn't have everything, so we went on to the Régie. They didn't have what he needed either, so we went to his house—like Mahouna's a room on a courtyard shared by many families. He pointed out his wife squatting over a fire in the courtyard with their baby on her back and located what he wanted in a toolbag under the bed. On the way back in the car he kept saying, "I don't want to leave you without water tonight" and "You can't quit a job for lack of a part."

He rigged up a pipe outside the house wall to bypass one inside that must have become blocked while the water was turned off and connected it where I used to have an outside tap. This arrangement is supposedly temporary, until the Caisse replaces the inside pipe. Likewise, masons from the Régie are supposed to come and patch the pavement in my driveway. But there are two other apartments in this block with scars in their driveways. I expect the bypass will stay, signature of the plumber who bypassed bureaucracy.

I didn't know how much money my new "little brother" would expect from his "big sister," but I had noticed when we went to the village that René slipped his cousin 5,000 francs, so I gave the head plumber 5,000 to share with his crew. Money is a kind of language here that nobody teaches but you need to know. If you hang on to it too tightly you're stingy, and if you part with it too easily you're a sucker. And it's hard to know where the dividing line is. But in this case I felt that even if I gave too much it was okay; exuberance was the spirit of the day. The crew wanted to know when they'd be able to see the pictures. I said it would take about a month to get them developed and they'd be slides so I couldn't give them copies. That was okay, they'd come back to visit me in a month.

Meanwhile, when the water was restored and the considerations had been exchanged, there were five muddy men and a pile of shovels and pipes in my driveway that I suddenly realized it was my responsibility to take home. So I spread the shower curtain I'd replaced over the back seat of the car, and we fitted the tools into the hatch and drove back to the Régie.

When I returned, René's car was in the driveway. He'd stopped by after tennis to ask if I'd like to attend a labor history seminar he's organizing in Kpalimé this weekend. Veterans of the labor movement are going to talk about their experiences of the founding of unions under colonialism and their consolidation into one government-run union under Eyadéma. The purpose is both to introduce contemporary union leaders to their forefathers and to record oral history for the archives of the labor education center. The seminar starts on Wednesday, but René would pick me up on Thursday when he has to come back to Lomé for something anyway. When the seminar was over on Saturday, we could go sightseeing in the Kpalimé region. This looks like the moment of truth, but the chance to be in on this oral history is unmissable, so I said yes. We'll see what happens. I asked René to reserve two rooms; he looked a little startled, but agreed.

Labor History Seminar

✉ ✉ ✉ ✉ ✉ ✉ ✉ ✉

It's siesta time at the labor history seminar in Kpalimé. I'm in my room in the Grand Hôtel du 30 Août, named for the date in 1969 when Eyadéma proclaimed the single national party, the Rassemblement du Peuple Togolais, or RPT, which is both the sponsor of the seminar and an antagonist in the stories the veterans have been telling.

René and I arrived yesterday afternoon in the middle of the last (and I gather best) of the veterans' reminiscences. A wiry little man in a white suit, whom the others called *le doyen*, was acting out his experience of the conflict in 1972 and '73 when Eyadéma insisted that the two unions forged in colonial days merge into one as part of the RPT. As the *doyen* explained it now, in this government-sponsored seminar, the unions were for unity but not for a complete abdication of autonomy. The skirmishes between labor leaders and soldiers, holdouts and sellouts, sounded as though they could have been taking place between the fledgling labor movement and the colonial government in the 1940s. The *doyen*'s stories of the personal impact of political conflict—jobs lost, families starved out, friendships betrayed—reminded me of Ousmane Sembene's novel *God's Bits of Wood*, where the railroad workers' antagonist is the French colonial government. The *doyen* managed to convey both the passion of the moment and the irony of retrospect. When he got to the point where he, a holdout for labor autonomy, hid under the bed from soldiers, he got up and crawled under the speakers' table, emerging by degrees, talking all the time, as the soldiers dragged him out. It was a magnificent performance; everybody laughed and clapped helplessly.

I tried to get René to explain how a single government-controlled union could have any leverage, particularly when most jobs are in government-controlled industries or for government contractors, but I didn't get an answer I could understand. He said that the result of consolidation is that there are now three parties to any labor dispute—management, union, and government—and (therefore?) strikes are seldom necessary.

There are fifteen participants in the seminar. Besides René, the organizers include a couple of officers of the union (the CNTT, Confédération Nationale des Travailleurs Togolais), and René's counterparts from the labor education center in Dakar—a young gallant named Alioune and his older colleague Moustapha. The rest of the group is about evenly divided between veterans and young union officers. The moment we walked into the meeting room, I realized I had to forge a role for myself. The only woman, the only non-African, the only one with no connection to the labor movement, I have no apparent role except that of "René's girlfriend," which I'm not ready to embrace. René introduced me as a teacher from the United States who wanted to learn about Togolese society and institutions to better teach my students. I said how privileged I felt to be there and that I hoped to contribute by taking photographs, which I would give to the labor center. In fact, I am turning out to be the conference photographer because René is kept busy enough with the tape recorders.

At dinner last night, I seemed to be taken as "the American." The others asked whether I'd eaten Togolese food before and whether I liked it. The *doyen* told stories of his three visits to America. In Houston in 1960, he said, he and some other African labor leaders had been asked to leave a restaurant because the waitress said their presence was making the white patrons leave.

"Too bad you didn't speak English," Alioune observed, but the *doyen* corrected him. He knew that this had happened *despite* the fact that they were speaking French.

"Okay," he said, "we left, but I took the key to the restaurant and locked the lady in. She wanted to be left alone? I left her alone."

The police came, followed by the NAACP leadership. Finally the president of a black college invited the group to eat in the college dining hall. The *syndicalistes* were unwilling to give up the fight, but also reluctant to make things hard for the American blacks. In the end, they enjoyed participating in the year-end festivities at the college. The next day, the story was in the newspaper.

"But that was all a long time ago," the *doyen* added, as though to avoid misleading the young people (and embarrassing me). "Now it is not like that. America is a beautiful country."

He also remembered a Christmas he had spent with an American family. What impressed him was that everyone in the family, even the smallest children, gave everyone else a present, "even if it was only a *bic*." In Togo, parents give presents, children only receive. The next year, he instituted the American practice in his family; he thought it was good for children to learn to give.

Meanwhile, René at the other end of the table was exercising his diplomatic skills. He passed around pictures he'd taken at a conference some of these people had attended in Conakry. He drew out the shy members of the group, flattered the veterans, proposed toasts (drunk variously in beer, Malta, and tap water, which I discovered after I'd drunk a lot of it was what the mineral-water bottles on the table contained), and managed to be the patron and the respectful youth at the same time.

By breakfast this morning, I had become "the woman." The other men ribbed René about working day *and* night, which he must have found ironic. After breakfast, a professional photographer arrived to take group photos outside under the conference banner. After he had taken all the official poses, I handed him my camera and asked him to take a group picture with me in it; the men cheered and called me *la fleur*, a name that has stuck.

Then while a small committee edited the proceedings in preparation for the closing session this afternoon, the labor center van took the rest of us shopping and sightseeing in town. Kpalimé is to some degree foreign territory to nearly everyone here. Alioune is a thousand miles from home. He wanted to buy souvenirs at the artisanal center. Some of the men are from distant parts of Togo. One man from Tabligbo wanted to visit his son in a *lycée* here. Even those from this area are from villages and have limited opportunity to get to a city. Most of them had errands at a doctor's office, the hospital, or Togopharma; the labor center was treating them to any medications they might need, and they seemed to need a lot. The men without specific errands were as interested as I in seeing the *lycée*, the hospital, the Koranic school, and the artisanal center. And they were as unable as I to talk with the woodcarvers and batik designers who didn't speak French. Suave junior executive Alioune did remind me though of our cultural differences. He bought two identical macramé handbags—one for each wife. If they were the least bit different, he explained, each wife would think the other's was better.

By the time we returned to the hotel for lunch, I had been admitted to a nonexclusive category, "the youth." The *doyen* asked me how old I thought he was. I guessed low on purpose, but was much farther off than I'd thought. He is seventy-five. Others chimed in, and soon we were in the midst of a general age-guessing game. It turns out that more of the group are veterans than I realized; several of the men look twenty years younger than they are. They were wrong about me, too, though. In Togo it's hard to imagine a single woman of thirty-six.

On the Town
⊠ ⊠ ⊠ ⊠ ⊠

Most of the seminar delegates left after the closing session this afternoon, and René, Alioune, and I went out to dinner at the Concordia, Kpalimé's other (and lesser) hotel. When we asked about dinner, the desk clerk looked dubious and went out to consult with someone. He returned to say we could have steak, green beans, and *frites* (French fries), but the beans would take an hour to cook. We stayed—René and Alioune wanted to escape the seminar stragglers, and Kpalimé's only other restaurant was closed. When the food came (tough steak, stringy beans, dry *frites*), we asked for napkins. The desk-clerk-doubling-as-waiter again looked distressed. He withdrew and returned with three pillowcases; they were out of napkins because the washman was sick. We shared a tissue from my purse and left the pillow-cases folded.

After dinner we went out to the patio to join the dancing. The patio was enclosed by a rush fence and lit with strings of colored lights. In one corner, a couple of young men tended the record player and the drinks cooler. Tables were set around the periphery.

The whole atmosphere was surreal. René was distracted. I couldn't get the hang of the dance rhythms. Every time I looked at Alioune, I thought of his twin macramé handbags. I began to notice that almost all the dancers were men, while chubby teenage girls sat on the sidelines in threes and fours trying to make bottles of Fanta last. René explained that the men were dancing with each other because if they asked a woman to dance, they'd have to pay for her drink, which they couldn't afford. A couple of these male couples dressed and moved and hung over each other pretty suggestively. Wasn't it possible that some of them were gay? No, insisted René, homosexuality doesn't exist in Togo. Alioune kept his eyes on the dancers.

When the dance floor had filled up, a little man came sliding in on his knees. You see quite a few people with shriveled legs in Togo, some from polio, some they say from misplaced injections that hit the sciatic nerve. The lucky few have hand-propelled tricycles; others propel themselves on wooden platforms with roller-skate wheels or drag themselves around on wooden blocks strapped to their hands. They sit with their legs folded under them at intersections in Lomé where drivers stopped at a red light can't escape their imploring gestures.

At first I thought this man had come to beg. But no, he'd come to dance. He twisted his torso to the rhythm, his head at the height of other dancers' thighs. He looked painfully vulnerable, but the others made way for him and danced facing him for short periods before turning back to their partners. He beamed up at these temporary partners and they smiled down at him. The man with shriveled legs seemed more at home at the dance than the girls clutching their soft drinks or René or Alioune or I.

The Plateau

✉ ✉ ✉ ✉

Yesterday, after the last of the conference delegates left, René and I drove up onto the Danyi Plateau. We stopped first in the Kpalimé market to buy yams, avocados, and oranges to take back to Lomé. Kpalimé is the market town for Togo's fruit basket; whenever city people travel to Kpalimé, they take back a trunkload of produce. In both Lomé and Kpalimé the Grand Marché includes a three-story concrete block building and the surrounding streets. In Lomé, the surrounding streets are a congested grid. In Kpalimé, they meander a little; grass and bushes grow in neglected spots; the whole atmosphere is more relaxed. It had rained Friday night, the weeds were still wet, people were buying sweet bread for breakfast, and the vendors seemed to be conserving their energy for busier times. At every corner René stopped to greet someone he'd grown up with. We bought our oranges from a cousin of his whose table was in a row with three other vendors, each with the same oranges at the same price and, I suppose, her own clientele of kin.

In the morning we took the road west from Kpalimé into the hills at the southern end of the plateau to visit the Château Viale and the Campement de Kloto. The château is a most improbable Norman-looking gray stone castle on a hilltop overlooking the Ghana border. It was built by a Frenchman during World War II and is now being renovated as a weekend retreat for the president, a kind of unrustic Camp David. The road up to the château was blocked by a log at a point where we couldn't see the building, so we got out and hiked up a rocky road in the sun not knowing how far we'd have to walk or whether we'd be allowed to look around once we got there. But it was only about half a mile to the top, where we found a caretaker prepared to give tours. He recited the château's history and showed us one of the renovated rooms, which could have been in any

51

Sheraton. There was a certain drama in seeing a room that might later be slept in by the obsessively protected president. The prohibition against photographing anything connected with the president is a source of income for the young men hanging out with the guide. One of them led me out of sight of the others and pointed out that I could take a picture of the château if I pretended to be shooting the scenery and then quickly turned to the château. I grabbed my clandestine shot, but then wished I hadn't because I discovered I didn't have appropriate change. The guide got mad and, wifelike, I had to ask René for money. The scenery was really more compelling than the château. You looked out over the stone wall across a field of wildflowers to green slopes, gradually bluing hills, and the shimmer of Lake Volta.

We had lunch nearby at the Campement de Kloto, a kind of hill station with cabins and an artisanal center. The *campement* has the feel of a summer camp in the White Mountains and, as a place to stay in a forest, serves almost the role of a state park. Lunch—sliced avocado in vinaigrette, grilled chicken with fresh tomato sauce, *ignames frites* (French fries made from rugged, starchy yams), and a choice of oranges or bananas for dessert—was served on the verandah of the main building. It's hard to overstate the luxury of a simple meal on a cool porch looking out into trees. We lingered afterward on shady paths carpeted with leaf mold. René says when you stay here overnight you need blankets.

After lunch we headed up to the highest part of the plateau, where there is a Benedictine monastery. The Danyi Plateau isn't very high, about three thousand feet at most, but it rises steeply from the central plain. As soon as we turned west off the Kpalimé-Atakpamé highway, we were on a mountain road. The bush turned to forest; the air freshened; at every switchback, the plain fell farther away and the slopes looked steeper and deeper green. I suddenly understood the connection between the geographical and emotional meanings of *relief*. After flat, dusty, daily Lomé, long deep green vistas and sharp slopes were another country.

When the song "Salade de Fruits" came on the radio, René grinned at me and sang along, "Salade de fruits, jolie, jolie . . ." Imagine me being courted by a popular song comparing a creole maiden to a fruit salad—and liking it.

At the top of the plateau, the terrain leveled to rolling, and the forest gave way to cultivated fields and savannah. We passed neat villages of rectangular mud-brick houses. Patches of red peppers drying on the shoulder brightened the road. People sitting under trees in the packed-clay yards or walking along the roadside looked up and waved.

The Dzobégan monastery is an oasis of order and productivity. It seems to be the fulfillment of the commandment "cultivez votre jardin." It is in fact an experimental and educational farm, but the sense of cultivation comes not only from the neatly fenced fields of corn and pasture, shady mango groves, and coffee-covered slopes but from evidence everywhere that the community makes the best of what's available. The cloisters curve toward a verandah supported by native teak posts and shaded by bougainvillea. The octagonal chapel is built of native woods and furnished with local carving. The high windows all around like a clerestory let in light all day; where the sunlight falls, the wood glows golden. In a country where garbage piles up in the streets and fields are cleared by burning, a place like Dzobégan is a powerful restorative, a vision of what could be. You just know the monks compost their garbage.

At the gift shop, we bought honey and coffee and a cassette of "Chants des Moines de Dzobégan." On one side is the "Office de Matin," on the other "Interludes de Kora." We drove back down the mountain with the *kora* interludes on the tape deck at the magic late afternoon hour when the sun turns mud brick and yellow stucco to rose and gold and drying peppers to rubies. The *kora* is a deep-bellied lute made from a gourd. Among the selections, I recognized "Jésu, Joy of Man's Desiring." As we wound down the switchbacks, the clear plucked treble and rolling resonant bass sang the feel of the road and the sun dappling through the trees and the deep tranquillity of the afternoon.

By the end of the day, I'd caught up to René, and it was easy to share his room. We meandered home today, stopping at the weaving center in Assahoun, and for lunch at Bethania, a combination farm, resort, and Protestant mission as thriving in a more worldly way as Dzobégan. It was a lovely weekend.

Ecole des Lettres
☒ ☒ ☒ ☒ ☒ ☒

The Ecole des Lettres is gearing up for the start of classes next Monday. For the past two weeks we've been giving make-up exams to students who failed last June.

The entire school of letters, which includes the departments of philosophy, history, German, social sciences, and "lettres modernes" (that is, French), as well as English, is housed in a one-story, U-shaped building with a porch all around the outside where students congregate. There are usually a couple of motorcycles parked up near the porch and half a dozen cars—Alf Storey's Civic, Madame Yamajako's Toyota, Dagadou's *deux chevaux*—where their owners think the shade of a tree might fall. Three classrooms open onto the porch at the bottom of the U; the legs have interior corridors with departmental offices and mailboxes. There are no individual offices. The English Department office is perhaps twelve feet square; it's hard to judge because it's lined with bookcases, stacks of boxes, and shelves heaped with dusty piles of papers. In the center, three small metal desks are pushed together to make a table. There are three chairs, one high stool, and two file cabinets, no typewriter, no telephone. This week the office has had the air of a command center from which Dagadou dispatches his corps of exam givers. He's far too busy with exams to think about what my third course should be.

The exam structure assumes that the exams themselves are objective and anticipates bias in their administration. The word for "proctor" sets the tone: "invigilate." Students don't know until the last minute whether the exam in a particular course will be written or oral. Professors invigilate each other's exams and grade blind. The completed exams are sent somewhere, Dagadou wasn't clear about where, as a permanent record for academic standards. Theoretically, two faculty members invigilate each exam to check on each other, but I gave two by myself; there aren't enough professors to go around. For one written and one oral exam, I was paired with Miss Messan, the Togolese American literature professor, who, though she prefers to speak French, is for some reason always called Miss. Dagadou implied that he got so many complaints about her that it would be unwise to let her give an exam alone. Though they don't know me, people seem to assume that *I* will be impartial and see things their way.

I met Miss Messan for the first time when she arrived at the written exam. Her face was pulled tight by a spiral of corn rows that culminated in a kind of horn at the crown, and she seemed wary of me. She gave the directions (in French) and I passed out the scrap paper—one thin green sheet per student. After a few students came up to the desk for a second sheet, the ration Dagadou had given us was gone.

The oral exam was for Miss Messan's own American literature course. We got started late because she assumed I was providing the questions and we had to make them up on the spot. She wrote the five questions on separate pieces of paper and folded them up. The students waited outside the room and came in one by one to draw a question and prepare while the previous student was answering. Grading is theoretically on a scale of 20, with 10 passing, but it's considered bad form to give grades over 14. People joke that 16 is for the teacher's pet, 18 for the teacher, and 20 for God. Miss Messan was trying to impress me with her high standards and at the same time make herself agreeable to the American who probably was an easy grader, and I was trying to fit into the way things are done here, so we agreed fairly readily on the grades. I would have had to design and grade the written exam for third-year American literature students if Flint hadn't passed them all last June—very bad form indeed.

This morning I assisted another faculty member with the oral exam for the second-year language course. Mr. Djoliba is as different as possible from Miss Messan. Tall, loose-limbed, affable, in T-shirt and jeans, he reminded me of a high-school basketball coach. For this exam, the students could select any of the five topics Mr. Djoliba had designated. No one chose the question on which I've seen so many freshman essays, "Has sport any real value?" Only one student addressed the question on the educational value of travel. People don't usually like traveling, he said, despite the proverb "He who travels is wise."

The students who answered the question "If you could live anywhere in the world during any historical period, where and when would you prefer to live?" all chose some moment in African history. One wanted to live in West Africa in the second half of the sixteenth century when the slave trade started. He would set up an army to fight the chiefs who sold slaves and the Europeans who bought them. Another wanted to be a king's page in seventeenth-century Abomey (the seat of the kings of Dahomey from about 1600 to 1900) so he could see the legendary juju and atrocities with his own eyes.

The most popular question, and the one most of the women chose, was "Can the problem of jealousy between wives be solved?" The common answer was that jealousy is inevitable in polygamy and can only be eradicated by monogamy. One woman said that if the husband wants many wives, he must take the consequences. Another said that a man cannot stick to one woman. The best thing for a woman to do is to stay in a corner and be satisfied no matter what her husband does. That was certainly better than leading a solitary life as some Western women did. One man recounted a story from his own *quartier* in Sokodé of a woman who poisoned her husband because he sat and chatted with his other wife and left her alone with her children.

This afternoon, we had an EDL faculty meeting. The unpopular *directeur* presided, after being introduced by his secretary, as though to distance or protect him from the faculty crowded and trapped in seats like bleachers with desks. The faculty here has no legislative power, so the meeting was not structured by parliamentary procedure, but the topic was familiar, the criteria for tenure and promotion. The secretary read new regulations formulated by the administration, which is to say the government: Henceforth, a Ph.D. is required for tenure; publications are required for promotion; no new faculty members will be appointed without the Ph.D. Most professors do not have the Ph.D., for which they have to get a fellowship to study abroad, usually in the United States or France. They may have an American master's or a French "doctorat du troisième cycle" (which those educated in the United States consider the equivalent of a master's and those educated in France consider the equivalent of a Ph.D.).

"Discussion" is a misnomer for what followed. One by one and in varying terms, faculty members said you can't hold up European standards of scholarship in Third World conditions. How can we publish when we have to teach three or four overload courses or take a second job to support ourselves? How can we publish when we have no room of our own at home and no office at the university? How can we publish when we have to travel to America or Europe to find an adequate library? How can we publish when we have no scholarly journals here and have to compete with people who have time, space, and libraries for access to European and American journals? After each objection, the *directeur* said something to the effect of "I understand and share the concern of my esteemed colleague, so-and-so, but . . ." Finally, one speaker offered the minimal practical suggestion of the defeated: At least, it should not be too difficult to put more chairs in the departmental offices. The response: See if you can find extra chairs in the classrooms when you need them.

Family Friend
⊠ ⊠ ⊠ ⊠ ⊠

René has been acting strangely. Two days after we returned from the plateau, he was supposed to come by after tennis and didn't. We spent most of
the next weekend together; he'd been "busy" the day he didn't show up. I
haven't heard from him since. I should be glad; it was his quick assumption
of commitment that scared me off. But I don't like being expected to adjust
as he blows warm and cold.

I was glad when Vera suggested that I go with Philippe to her cousin's
birthday party this past Saturday. Vera felt obliged to be represented, but
she couldn't go herself because she was working that night. I'd be doing her
a favor by going with Philippe, it would be interesting for me to attend a
Togolese party, I wouldn't be sitting home pining for René, and with good
old family friend Philippe I could relax and have fun without worrying
about unexpressed expectations.

The party turned out to be a disappointment. Each group of guests
shook hands with the hosts, shook hands around the circle of sofas and
chairs set out in the sandy courtyard, then sat down and stuck fast through
dinner served at our seats. No one mixed; I couldn't even get a conversation
going with the woman sitting beside me. But between courses and after
dinner we danced on a concrete platform in the corner of the yard. Philippe
taught me the highlife. He's a good dancer and a good teacher, and the
basic step is easy, so the evening began to be fun, and when he suggested
we leave the stiff company and go to a nightclub, I was ready.

He took me to a funkier place than the international disco I'd been to
with René. The highlife beat and the aroma of barbecue and sweat promised
a good time. But as soon as we were installed in a dark corner, Philippe
revealed why he'd wanted to come to La Cachette ("the hiding place")
instead of staying in the company of his wife's family. Since he *is* a friend I

want to keep, I tried to explain why I couldn't possibly accept advances from my friend's husband. But I might as well have been speaking Martian. So much for simple fun.

Classes start tomorrow, and I've never been so ready.

FRIDAY, OCTOBER 21

First Week of School
⊠ ⊠ ⊠ ⊠ ⊠ ⊠ ⊠

Theoretically, classes started on Monday. But we didn't get our schedules till that morning and Dagadou had me down for two courses that met at the same time—the second-year Introduction to British and American Literature that Lee Ann was so anxious for me to teach and one of the two C1 (third-year specialization) courses in American lit. He had simply copied last year's schedule with different names, without realizing that Flint had not taught the British and American lit course. Dagadou didn't know what he could do about the conflict. He said he'd get "someone else" to teach the second-year course. But he doesn't have enough staff to cover all the courses as it is, let alone anyone who does both British and American lit. Meanwhile, he kept telling me he didn't know if I'd have any students in the C1 because I was unknown and Miss Messan, who teaches the third American lit course, was unpopular. At first, I'd worried that Dagadou would try to take advantage of me to fill in his staff shortages; now I wondered if I'd have anything to do at all. He suggested we wait and see whether I had a C1 class before doing anything about the schedule conflict. He would give me time at a meeting of all third-year students at five o'clock that afternoon to describe the courses I was offering and encourage students to take American literature.

So I went home and worked up a plug for my courses and returned before five. No one was around. I finally found Dagadou. "Oh," he said, "everyone was here at three, so we had the meeting then. But I spoke for you. I told the students that last year the American professor passed everyone. Five signed up."

He went on: Why didn't I put up a sign asking all students interested in American literature to come to a meeting on Wednesday afternoon, the time set aside for sports and activities, to arrange the hours? That didn't sound very promising, but there was nothing else to do.

60

In fact, the students did see the sign, and about eight came to the meeting. They were enthusiastic about taking American literature and willing to change the Thursday morning class to Wednesday morning, difficult because they have classes virtually all day every day except for the sacred Wednesday afternoon. Then we had to get a room for the class. A student took me to the office that schedules rooms. A room was found. So I have three classes, and I've learned that anything I want done I'd better do myself.

Thursday morning I met the second-year class as scheduled. The students were spread out in a large lecture hall; the side doors were open to the roar of motorcycles pulling up and parking outside, and I didn't know how well the students understood English, so I felt the struggle to communicate. I introduced myself as Ms. Blake and explained the significance of "Ms." Some of the students responded to the novelty and logic of a title for women that did not specify marital status.

I explained that, illogically enough, we would have to start the study of British and American literature with American, since we had an American literature anthology provided by the American Cultural Center but as yet no British materials. It seemed important to start with a reason for Togolese students to study American literature, so I gave a little lecture about American literature as a people's effort to define a national identity out of a colonial experience.

Then I assigned the snippets of Benjamin Franklin's autobiography for next week and distributed the books. Although the American Cultural Center provides the books for free, the English Department wants me to sell them to provide the start-up book fund that has not been allocated by the *directeur*. Ideally, the fund will perpetuate itself as books are sold to students. As soon as I announced that the books would cost 1,000 CFA ($2.50), the hands went up. We won't get our scholarship checks until the end of the month, the students said, could we please take the books on credit? Don't provide books on credit, Dagadou had warned me, you'll never see the money. But I can't have a class if the students don't read the material, the books won't do anybody any good in the trunk of my car, and they were after all donated, so I said okay. Of the twenty-five students, three or four paid; the rest signed a list, which is, by the way, my only class list for the course.

Finding materials for the British part of the course will be a challenge. There is no university bookstore, and the library fits into a classroom. The British Council left Lomé years ago. The department has multiple copies of some books, but not enough of anything except *The Reader's Digest Book of Short Stories*, which is used in the first-year course. The Shakespeare course this term will be on *Henry V*, period, because that's what the department has enough copies of. I've already asked Alf Storey, the British Council representative, who teaches English as a foreign language, for help, but his private library runs to Somerset Maugham.

The worst of it is that if the department had told me before I left what they needed, and if the USIA had told me that the Fulbrighter's announced limit of four boxes of books sent through the diplomatic pouch did not apply to Togo, I could have gotten publishers to donate enough unsold copies of superceded anthologies to keep the department in British and American literature for years. Of all the shortages in Togo, the most frustrating is the shortage of information.

Housewarming
⊠ ⊠ ⊠ ⊠ ⊠

Last night I had a party for everyone I knew in Lomé, and a few I didn't. Vera's long-term houseguest Mercy, here from Ghana trying to set herself up as a caterer, did the food—chicken and beef brochettes, fried yam and plantain, yam balls, a bean dish, a rice dish, and fruit salad. I contributed the all-American veggies and dip. Mahouna came to answer the door, keep the cooler supplied with drinks, and grill the brochettes (on a local "coal-pot" down in the carport). René brought his boombox and a stack of tapes.

Everyone said it was a great success. In the morning I'd encountered Lee Ann's French friends, Jacques-Alain and Marie-France, at the pool and invited them. Since most of the guests were Americans, I was afraid the others might feel a little peripheral. But Jacques-Alain and Philippe recognized each other from their English class at the American Cultural Center and appreciated the prod to get acquainted. Kay and the Storeys, who have age and the teaching of English as a foreign language in common, had been hearing about each other for a long time but never met. Everyone said, oh, what a good idea to have African food, made a note of Mercy's name for their own future parties, and marveled that I'd settled in and made friends so quickly.

But I was aware that all the people there, except Kay, were settled in their own worlds and, while happy to go to parties, not interested in developing new relationships. The Americans my age have a social group centered around the American School. My Togolese colleagues are enmeshed in their extended families. Elise telephoned today to apologize for not coming; in the midst of a family gathering, she'd forgotten. Lee Ann brought her husband—and had to leave early because he doesn't like parties. Kay is generous and loyal but unhappy in her job and uninterested in Togo, so a good friend but a limited companion.

And René has moved on to the newest female American in town. When I set the date for the party, a week after we returned from Kpalimé, I kind of knew I'd better hurry up and have it or I wouldn't feel like it. There'd been the time he didn't come by when he said he would, and another day I'd seen him driving on the Boulevard Circulaire with a woman in the car. (Lomé is such a small town—only a fraction of its 350,000 people drive cars, play tennis, shop at SGGG—that there's no hiding place.) I met the woman, Sharon, a recent college graduate here as a bank intern, at a reception last week, and she claimed her territory: "René talks about you a lot; I think he has a lot of respect for you." A few days later, I met her again at the embassy cashier, and figuring, what's done is done and I might as well know for sure, invited her to the party. She came and they behaved like a couple. At the same time René claims "nothing has changed" and he's good friends with both of us.

As people were leaving, Sharon said, "René and I and Vera and Philippe are going dancing. Come with us."

I said, no thanks, I have to take Mercy and Mahouna home.

It turned out that Mahouna had brought his bicycle, and we could drop Mercy off on the way downtown. Vera and Sharon said "Oh, come on." And I said to myself, okay, be a good sport, and gave in.

René and Sharon left in his car, and I took Vera, Philippe, and Mercy. When we got to the club, René was alone. He said Sharon had said she had a sore throat and insisted on being taken home. "I don't know what it is with you two," he said, and I was reminded of what Mr. Djoliba's students had said about polygyny: A man who takes more than one wife has to take the consequences, and a woman should stay in a corner and be satisfied no matter what her husband does. I danced a couple of dances with René, who was distant and disappointed, and one with Philippe, who pressed his suit and a few other things, and then I said I was tired and left, glad I had my own car.

One man of my acquaintance has proved true. Mahouna appeared this morning, unasked, to help clean up.

Then I took *Mansfield Park*, borrowed from Kay, to the pool and spent the afternoon in sympathetic company.

Second Week of School

✉ ✉ ✉ ✉ ✉ ✉ ✉ ✉

I thought all my administrative problems were solved when I met my American lit class for the first time last Monday. Twelve students showed up—exactly the number of books I have and of trustworthy seats (out of twenty-four) in the classroom. I meet this class twice a week for two hours. I've divided the time into a year-long course on the American Dream in American Literature and two one-semester courses, one on American poetry, the other on American women writers. The students were responsive when I asked what they associated with the term "American Dream"; we seemed to understand each other's English; and there were enough different responses to generate a discussion.

So I was feeling good when I dropped by the English Department after class to see if there was anyone there to talk to. Only Dagadou. He said, "Oh, by the way, we've decided to change the second-year course in English and American literature to an elective in English lit alone."

I'm not sure who "we" is, but at any rate I now need to come up with some British literature immediately.

Tuesday I had lunch with Lee Ann, who told me she had left a stencil for "Sir Gawain and the Green Knight" in the bottom drawer of the file cabinet in the English Department. Right after lunch I went to the department office, found the stencil in the midst of an inky heap, and begged the EDL mimeo lady to let me have copies by Thursday morning.

In class Thursday, I collected *Highlights of American Literature*, refunded what money had been paid, and distributed "Sir Gawain." I was embarrassed to be the agent of such an arbitrary switch, but the students were unperturbed. Their only problem was that there weren't enough copies of "Gawain" to go around because another twenty-five students had shown up.

Meanwhile, Kay has put me on the planning committee for an in-service training seminar for all *lycée* English teachers to be held in Atakpamé just before Christmas. The other members of the committee are Dagadou, Elise, and four English teachers from *lycées* in Lomé. We had a working dinner at Kay's last week, and it was painful.

In the first place, Kay's hospitality can be oppressive. One of the teachers is a quiet, philosophical vegetarian. Kay kept telling him that the groundnut stew she served was "good for him" because it contained hard-boiled eggs—never mind that it's based on beef. Dagadou tried to pass up Clarence's favorite dessert, a whipped gelatin affair studded with pineapple chunks, walnuts, and miniature marshmallows. Kay insisted he take some, kept after him until he ate a few bites, and made us all agree that yes, it was light and cool and therefore the perfect dessert.

In the second place, it became clear that the planning committee has no real function. The government requires attendance at the seminar. The American Cultural Center sponsors it. Kay does the actual organization. Peace Corps volunteers involved in TEFL lead the workshops on teaching techniques. Kay kept asking the teachers what language-teaching topics they wanted covered and what they thought should be on the program, but they're going to get what the available Americans have to offer regardless. The only Togolese on the program is Elise, who is to give a plenary lecture on the application of linguistics to language teaching. In effect, the role of the planning committee is to pretend that the teachers have asked for what they're obliged to accept.

I'm to give the other plenary lecture. About this, the Togolese teachers *have* had a say. They want me to discuss "the situation of blacks in the United States *actuellement*." "*Actuellement*" means "at the present time." The most recent text on civil rights or race relations in their materials for the *terminale* course on American Civilization is Martin Luther King's 1963 "I Have a Dream" speech, so they're right to want an update. But to my English ear, *actuellement* still implies "really," and I can't help wondering who am I to explain "the situation of blacks in the United States *really*." To teach black literature in the United States—with black students and colleagues and within the American racial dynamic—is one thing; to represent black American experience to Africans is quite another.

This week I've also started French conversation sessions with Alidou, the California students' tutor. He's one of the legion of unemployed university graduates here, which most of my students will join in a couple of years. He supports himself by teaching French and African culture for the Peace Corps—a seasonal job—and giving private French lessons. He's very nice and very professional. He roared up on his motorcycle ten minutes early and wouldn't accept a Coke until the session was nearly over. The conversation-starting questions he asked were "Do you believe in God?" and "Why do you Americans waste so much food?"

He understood why the second question bothered me. It's from a list of about fifty "*questions de choc*" in the Peace Corps language-teaching materials. When I got through sputtering that *I* didn't waste food, it led to a discussion of the psychology of affluent children of Depression-raised parents, something the Togolese haven't had to think about yet, and the economics of stockpiling food to raise the price, which sounds pretty crass in Togo.

The other question was Alidou's own, and he didn't think of it as shocking. He is Muslim and does believe in God, as well as in the continued participation of the dead in the lives of the living. I wanted to hear about his beliefs, which are clear, rather than talk about mine, which aren't. But he was determined that his job was to make me talk.

Junior Year Abroad
✉ ✉ ✉ ✉ ✉ ✉ ✉

Last night Britt and Amy, two of the California students, took Alidou and me to dinner at Sous les Manguiers ("under the mango trees"), a student restaurant in the courtyard of a private home near the university. For 200 francs, you get a generous plateful of *pâte* and meat or fish sauce doled out by the cooks in a kerosene lamp–lit lean-to and take it to one of the low candle-lit tables set in the sand. The food is good. Forks are offered to *yovos* and a basin of water to those who use their hands. Those who don't want to risk the *eau glacé* can bring bottled soft drinks. The carpet of sand and curtain of darkness around each circle of candlelight muffle sound and create a gracious and intimate atmosphere. The place is a find—literally; you'd have to live nearby or be a student to know it existed.

Best of all, this is a place that cuts across the differences in resources that can make relationships so awkward here—cheap enough for Britt and Amy to afford and not to embarrass Alidou, obscure enough to be a treat for me that only students could provide and therefore to reciprocate for the dinners they've eaten at my house. They are so determined to be self-sufficient that they hesitate to suggest outings or even contact me because they don't want to appear to be asking for a ride or inviting themselves to dinner. This adds to the difficulty of communication, because without telephones, the only way I have to reach them is to leave a note in one of the general alphabetical pigeonholes in the EDL or to drive, over the cratered track, through the sand trap and the schoolboys' soccer game, to the villa (private home leased by the university for student housing) where they live with ten other women. But I know how they feel because much as I love retreating to Kay's air-conditioned haven for lunch, I hate the way she always provides, always pays, always turns an invitation to her into one from her. So I'm grateful for Sous les Manguiers.

Britt and Amy are the survivors of the four students I met in SGGG the day I arrived. One gave up and went home after their six-week French course and before the university opened. The other, Barbara, the black woman who was taking charge, has effectively quit going to classes and is on the verge of moving into an apartment provided by her Fulani boyfriend. Barbara is turning out to be as much of a foreign experience for Britt and Amy as Togo is. She met Beaugosse (who they all assume is married) the first week, and so close were the California students that she took the others along on her dates. Beaugosse would pick them all up in his Mercedes and take them to such exotic places as the restaurant of the Deux Février, where dinner for five would cost most of a civil servant's monthly salary. The fact that they were eating cassava with pepper and gristle in the refectory of the *lycée*, where they lived during the French course, added to the unreality and allure of these excursions. They sometimes sat in the backseat of the car while tiny packages and big money changed hands in the front. "Il fait le commerce," explains Amy in the cryptic style she's picked up from their African housemates. Diamonds, suspects Britt, mined in Sierra Leone and smuggled throughout West Africa.

Britt finds Barbara and her life thrilling. She's emerging for the first time from a bookish life (no books to bury yourself in here) ravenous for experience. For her, riding in the backseat of the Mercedes is like watching an international crime thriller from almost inside the film. Barbara is a model of liberation, the existential woman, deliciously indifferent to the expectations of others. Her confidence is flattering, her advice possibly invaluable.

Amy is more troubled. What she wants most is to become part of a community with their African housemates. What Britt sees as Barbara's liberation, Amy considers self-dramatizing irresponsibility. She sympathizes with Barbara's timid, studious Nigerian roommate, who is supposedly the reason Barbara is moving out of the villa. While Britt and Barbara take their mattresses up on the roof to sleep and gossip, Amy finds the roommate crying because she's afraid to sleep alone and takes *her* mattress into Barbara's room to keep the roommate company. Britt sees Barbara's relationship with Beaugosse as immersion in African life; Amy notices that the African women, serious students scraping by, keep their distance from Barbara and wonders if Barbara is one reason they are so wary of her and Britt. So, although Barbara is exciting and generous and gives them a glimpse of an aspect of African life they otherwise wouldn't see, she acts as a wedge between Britt and Amy and between them and their housemates.

All this is beneath the surface, however, and almost in the past. The farther Barbara strays from the prescribed path, the less Britt and Amy see of her, and they depend on each other too much to let their differences come between them. A junior year in Togo is a challenge.

They are the only white students, out of thirty-five hundred, at the university and the only white residents of their *quartier*. They feel like something of a sideshow. The neighborhood children run after them chanting the ditty all children seem to learn as soon as they can talk:

> Yovo, yovo,
> Bonsoir!
> Ça va bien?
> Merci!

Amy got sick of being called *yovo* and taught the kids who live near them to call her "Amy." Now they call both students "Aimée."

When they walk into a class, all eyes turn to them. They'll be struggling to follow a lecture in French well enough to take intelligible notes when the professor will suddenly ask, "And what do *les américaines* think about that?"

Amy tells a story of sitting in on a lecture during the first week of classes to see if she wanted to take the course. When the students thought the professor was speaking too fast (they take down the lectures like dictation), about fifty of them called out, "*Doucement*, monsieur, there's a *yovo* among us!" and burst into a chorus of "Yovo, yovo, Bonsoir!"

Housekeeping in the villa is strenuous. Britt and Amy have a tiny room—the smallest, they tell me, because it has a closet and "Africans think Americans need closets"—with two beds, a refrigerator (provided by their education abroad program), and just enough floor space to open the closet door. Since Britt sleeps on the roof, she keeps her mattress on the landing and they use the plywood platform of her bed for storage—books, toothbrushes, hot plate, dishes, powdered milk, detergent, all in a jumble.

The kitchen of the villa is used as a bedroom, so all the residents cook on hot plates in their own rooms. It's too much of an undertaking to get to SGGG or the Grand Marché very often, so Britt and Amy shop at a little neighborhood market and think of what is sold there—rice, yams, potatoes, onions, tomato paste, oranges, bananas—as all that's available. They have learned to like what is easiest to get and cook. Eggs and the seedy, tough-membraned local oranges are brought to the villa by a vendor. "We eat a lot of eggs," says Amy. "And I discovered the best lunch: leftover rice with bananas and milk. It only takes one bowl and with the bananas you don't taste the powdered milk so much." They're gratifying dinner guests, swoon over the simplest things: "Lettuce! Ice cream!"

"You know what the other girls do?" asks Britt. "We invited them to put whatever they wanted in our fridge, but most of them only keep water there. They make a big pot of something on the weekend and keep it under the bed. Everyday they bring it to the boil and eat some until it's gone."

Britt and Amy thought of hiring one of the eager neighborhood girls to do their laundry but realized that would separate them even more from their housemates. So they do it like everyone else, in cold water in buckets in the yard, hang it on the roof, and iron everything including underwear to kill the eggs of the mango fly, which if allowed to hatch on the skin, burrow into it and grow into painful boils.

"Remember when we used to think you had to change your sheets every week?" chortles Britt.

They're finding it difficult to get to know their housemates. Britt lived in an international house at Stanford and Amy in a sorority at Irvine; they think of their dorm as a kind of family and expected African life would be even more communal. But the African women are older and more independent than typical American college students. Some have children back home; many have live-in boyfriends; most keep to themselves. The villa's only communal activity is a Sunday evening gathering on the porch to braid hair and gossip, in which Britt and Amy feel like outsiders because they're considered too inexpert to braid hair, and they have trouble following the slangy conversation. They tell me about Rama, a "wise woman" (Britt's words) of indeterminate age who supports herself by selling cloth she imports from her home in Upper Volta and sometimes contributes her TV to the Sunday-evening porch gatherings; Ayélé, who has two children living with her mother in a village near Niamtougou and is very nice to Britt and Amy despite the fact that she seems to have less money than anyone; and especially Bernadette and Aminata, Ivoirians who live next door. They are a bit younger than the others, their boyfriends are back in Abidjan, and they too feel like foreigners. Amy especially likes Aminata, who she says is always calm.

Just recently Britt and Amy realized they are part of the reason the common areas of the villa have been so gritty, gummy, and maggotty. The other women didn't know how to assign cleaning duties to *yovos*, so they never allocated chores. Finally Amy got disgusted and attacked the bathroom and replaced a burned-out lightbulb. Then some of the others called a house meeting and drew up a list of chores and a rotation plan for doing them, but they still wouldn't let Britt and Amy sweep the yard. They didn't want the neighborhood to see the white women in their house doing menial labor. When Britt did it anyway, she said Ayélé came out to make sure her hands weren't getting calloused. Meanwhile, Amy points out, the men's dorms have maids.

While they're struggling to develop relationships with women, they're fighting off men. Male students ask where they live and propose to *rendre visite*. A professor they met with his wife at a Cultural Center reception invited them to lunch—at his house they assumed. When he picked them up, he said his wife was sick and drove them around all afternoon rendering visits to his male friends. Rama introduced them to her boyfriend's brother, who took a concerted interest in Amy and started rendering daily visits despite her efforts to discourage him. Amy was afraid the situation would alienate Rama, but instead it gave Aminata and Bernadette a way to show friendship. They started listening through the wall between their room and Rama's to find out when the brother was coming and then hiding Amy in their room when he came. Finally they convinced Rama to tell the brother to leave Amy alone. They surmise that Rama had some sort of financial arrangement with him. "Elle fait le commerce," observed Aminata.

While they find Barbara's relationship with the rich, handsome, suave, and shady Beaugosse exciting, the attention Britt and Amy attract is only—like the hot, dusty walk between villa and university—exhausting.

"It's such a *drag*," marvels Britt. "We can be covered with sweat and dirt and heat rash—"

"—which we usually are," adds Amy—

"—and downright insulting—"

"—which by now we always are—"

"—and they don't even notice. All they care about is that we're white."

"And yet the funny thing," muses Amy, "is that we all understood from the beginning that Beaugosse picked out Barbara because she's black. Or do you suppose it was Barbara that picked out Beaugosse?"

To stay healthy but not exploit your advantages, to be open to experience but not foolish, to be free of racism but not exploited for reasons of race—it's a tricky course. Their relationship with each other is not the least of the difficulties. Smart and resilient as they both are, they're very different. Britt is from a Seattle suburb, Amy a southern California farming town. Britt has a touch of Stanford snobbism; Amy state-school insecurity. Britt is quick, decisive, and sometimes sharp-tongued; Amy, considerate, understated, and sensitive to nuance. Britt grasps political relationships; Amy, personal ones. Britt craves experience; Amy reflects on its cost. It exacerbates their differences that almost everyone around them thinks of them as interchangeable. Yet the fact that everyone else is different enough from them to think that also binds them together.

And, in fact, their differences are really just different proportions of the shifting reactions all three of us have to living in a foreign world. I see myself in both of them. But their stories remind me of how insulated I am by an apartment, a car, and professor status, and I'm doubly impressed at how well they're getting along. They don't see their own success, though. They're both obsessed with their schoolwork—convinced that they don't understand enough of the lectures, won't be able to find materials for papers, won't be able to write in French, will fail their exams. I wonder if they're not focusing all the anxiety from other areas of life on the academic, because, ironically, it's the least important and hence safest to worry about.

Meanwhile, I'm itching to get away from the university, the Cultural Center, the usual faces and topics, and *do* something. I'm trying to persuade Britt and Amy to go on a three-day trip with me around the coffee-cocoa triangle—Kpalimé, Atakpamé, Badou. This would be a good time to go as the cocoa harvest is in progress. But their weekly meeting with their program director is Friday afternoon and they fear his wrath.

I also finally caught the elusive Steve Rosen—a Lafayette friend's Peace Corps buddy, now program director for AID—in his office and asked if I might go along as a photographer on trips to AID field projects. For a friend of a friend he was awfully cold, but he did admit that he knew they should be taking pictures and the last time he visited a project he'd slung a camera over his shoulder but had been too busy talking to people ever to use it. He gave me the description of a project near Lomé and said he'd pass on my offer to the project directors, who would call me if they were interested.

Literature without Books

☒ ☒ ☒ ☒ ☒ ☒ ☒ ☒ ☒

Between an anthology I found in the English Department and Kay's bookshelf, I've put together a syllabus for the first semester of British lit: my own abridgement of *Othello*, the first five chapters of *Pride and Prejudice*, and Shaw's *Arms and the Man*. The arbitrary start with "Sir Gawain" and what I think might be the students' interests have suggested a thematic focus on concepts of hero and heroine and myths of romantic love. To make multiple copies, I make one photocopy at the Cultural Center, from which Josèph, the technician, cuts a stencil on the electronic stencil cutter, which I then take to the EDL to be mimeographed. Getting the stencils cut is the weak link, because I have no right to ask anyone at the Cultural Center to do anything. I go through Kay, who travels a lot in her job and is therefore often not around to remind Josèph to get the job done. Last week when I went to pick up *Othello*, only the first act was done. A good thing it was, too. I had thought "Sir Gawain" would sustain us for two weeks, but Lee Ann's version is the barest plot summary; it has no imagery, no poetry, practically nothing to talk about except typographical errors. I was glad to have part of *Othello* to distribute for the next class.

Othello will go more slowly. Just distributing the copies has turned out to be a production. The EDL mimeograph lady doesn't collate copies, so I arranged the pages in piles around the edge of the lecturer's platform. The students immediately mobbed the platform, and I had to shout instructions to form a line. Then we had to sort out the effects of chaos: "Is anyone missing any pages? Who has more than one copy of page twelve?" In the end, fifty copies weren't enough. So today there was another distribution, of both *Othello* and "Sir Gawain," for newcomers to the class. One edge of every page of *Othello*, along the spine of the fat hardback anthology, is fuzzy, so I spent most of the rest of the period writing columns of the missing words on the board.

The students are amazingly tolerant of these organizational chores and greedy for instruction. I'd no sooner filled in the fuzzy words when someone asked why we weren't reading all of *Othello*. When we swapped *Highlights of American Literature* for "Sir Gawain" two weeks ago, I asked the class to spend the rest of the period writing about their concept of the ideal man in preparation for reading "Sir Gawain" as a fictional definition of a hero. Though I read and returned each paper with brief comments, several of the students asked me to take their papers back and correct the grammar. Others who joined the class later asked for the assignment and turned papers in today. It's not that they're afraid of missing credit—the only marks that count are those on their final exams; any writing done during the semester is just for practice. What they had to say about the ideal man was pretty predictable: He's strong, honest, handsome, believes in God, and takes care of his family.

I asked Britt and Amy what is done about textbooks in their courses. They say most of the professors distribute (or write on the board) a short bibliography of helpful texts. Systematic Britt took these bibliographies straight down to Walter ("Vahl-tare"), the biggest bookstore, and bought what she could find. But Britt knows that she can read better than she can comprehend lectures in French, and she can afford to spend a hundred dollars on four books if she thinks they'll help her get through the semester. The Togolese students who can't spend $2.50 on a book until they get their scholarships (about $50 a month) can't do that. Amy says that the reading for her education course is articles in journals in the School of Education library. The journals, donated, are all at least ten years old.

A few weeks ago at the Cultural Center, I met a recent graduate of the university who now teaches English at a *lycée* in Badou, about a hundred and fifty miles northwest of Lomé. Last Saturday he came to call on me. He has a *maîtrise* in Anglophone African literature and wants to go to the United States to pursue a Ph.D. in comparative African and Afro-American literature. He wanted to know what secondary works I would recommend on Afro-American literature. In the course of our conversation, it came out that he had read almost no primary works. Part of *Invisible Man* was all I could pin down. I don't think he was lazy. He was introduced to me as the star English major of a couple of years back, and he had trekked down from Badou to do something toward a most remote graduate program. I think his professors never stressed primary materials, partly because of an authoritarian education tradition, partly because books are so unavailable. I made him a list of major black American writers to look for in the American

Cultural Center library and gave, lent, or sold him some books. His chances of getting to study in the United States are remote because the American government distributes fellowships according to Togolese government priorities, and the Togolese government wants its current university faculty to get Ph.D.'s. So, at the moment, you have to teach at the university to get a fellowship, and have a Ph.D. to teach at the university.

Probably the best thing I did for the teacher from Badou was to give him a copy of the *Norton Introduction to Literature* as a source for his teaching. He was so grateful. His position—teaching without books, in a *lycée* as opposed to a junior high, in Badou as opposed to someplace more remote—is about the best my students have to look forward to. And it also reveals the high-school background they have had. Unless they lived in Lomé, where they had access to the French and American Cultural Center libraries, they probably never read a whole book before they came to the university. The texts they read in school, if their teacher had to copy from a source, were probably no more than a couple of pages long. I forgot to ask the teacher from Badou whether he had to copy his teaching texts onto the blackboard for his students to copy into their notebooks. Perhaps he has access to a typewriter and ditto machine.

Coffee-Cocoa Triangle
✉ ✉ ✉ ✉ ✉ ✉ ✉

I'm sitting on the terrace of the Hôtel Kapokier in Atakpamé waiting for Britt and Amy to come down to breakfast. In the end, they decided that, since they're now the only ones left in their study-abroad program, they could ask the director to change this week's meeting so we could have a three-day trip. We left Friday morning and drove to Atakpamé the long way via Kpalimé. This is the first time I've driven outside of Lomé myself. There are just enough little tricks to driving here—avoiding goats and potholes, turning on the windshield wipers on gravel stretches—to make it feel like an adventure.

The Kapokier ("kapok tree") is a second-class provincial hotel with four rooms and one toilet. All the other guests look to be Togolese businessmen. Our room ($14 for three) has the basics—two double beds (with lumpy kapok mattresses), an air conditioner, a sink, a shower, a tiny table, one overhead light, and just enough floor space to get around in. The water (cold) is on only from about six to nine morning and night. But the terrace is luxurious. Atakpamé sits in the bottom of a bowl fringed by teak woods, and the hotel is halfway up one side. The terrace spreads out over a soccer field and the steep, tree-lined, cobblestone road down into town. At seven in the morning, there's brisk pedestrian traffic—the churchbells started at six, and the roosters before that. I imagine the pedestrians without head-loads are going to church.

It's been a serendipitous trip. One of the reasons Britt and Amy decided to come is that they realized that both the Togolese women whom Peace Corps volunteer friends of friends of theirs had asked them to look up live on the triangle route. Friday afternoon we stopped in Amlamé, on the road between Kpalimé and Atakpamé, to visit Britt's contact, a young woman who lives with her father and six children between one and ten in a clean-swept compound on the edge of the town. When we drove up, a boy playing outside streaked in to tell his mother, and she came out with the other children beaming welcome, even before she learned who we were. When Britt told her we'd come to bring greetings from the Peace Corps volunteer, she was delighted but not astonished; she said she knew her friend would return to her somehow. We'd brought presents from the Kpalimé market—fake-gold earrings for Abena, school notebooks for the older children, and yams. The yams were the big hit. Each child picked up one or two—these are big hairy stumps, over a foot long and four or five inches in diameter—and danced them inside.

It was an easy visit, without any of the sense I had in René's cousin's village of being trapped by protocol. Abena and Britt exchanged news. Her father showed us their granaries and orange trees and told us that they'd lost the market for their oranges because the fruit-processing plant, Togofruit, had gone bankrupt and closed. We took pictures. They gave us a big basket of oranges. I felt we'd met on common ground and each of us had given something we had plenty of and received something we appreciated.

Yesterday, we took a day-trip from Atakpamé to Badou, near the Ghana border. The drive across the mountains—on a gentle roller coaster of good empty road—was lovely. It's drier here than on the Danyi Plateau, so the views are more open and the colors more varied. Dry-grass hillsides spread away on both sides, laced with green creek beds and patched occasionally with a crazy-quilt of corrugated iron roofs in varying shades of rust. A cross between northern California and Provence.

In Badou, we looked up Amy's older brother's Peace Corps girlfriend's friend Kayi, a single woman in her twenties who works in an office and shares a house with another working woman. Her roommate was away for the weekend, and she was glad to take the day to show us around her area. We went first to the market in Tomegbé, a little town about twelve kilometers south of Badou. By now, we've seen a lot of markets, but this one was especially colorful and intimate. The flats of smoked fish in more shapes than I knew existed and the rows of different colored beans in enamel basins of graduated sizes seemed to have been arranged by an artist. Britt was delighted with a purchase of about a quart of boiled chestnuts wrapped in a cocoyam leaf for 15 francs, or about 4 cents.

In the market, Kayi met a friend of hers who invited us to her house for a drink. Britt contributed her chestnuts, which tasted like unseasoned navy beans, and we spent a pleasant hour out of the sun watching the market traffic through the open doorway and talking with the woman and her husband and brother-in-law about how the economy was changing for the worse, because of low coffee and cocoa prices and drought, and social mores were changing for the better, for example to allow Kayi to remain unmarried and live away from her family, still a singular situation.

Then Kayi took us to a cocoa plantation owned by another friend of hers, who was equally welcoming. Like most cocoa plantations, this was a small family farm; the owner said he had two hectares, only part of it planted in cocoa, the rest in bananas, citrus, and cassava. The family lives in a red-dirt clearing surrounded by green groves. As we arrived, the planter was turning cocoa beans drying on a huge table set in the yard.

The small trees in the cocoa grove were neatly planted with just enough space between to sun-dapple the crunchy curled-up leaves underfoot. I'd never thought about how cocoa grew—in green, yellow, and red ribbed pods, like elongated muskmelons, that hang directly from the trunk and major branches. It's a labor-intensive crop. When the pods are ripe, the beans, twenty or so per pod, and the pulp around them are scraped out and fermented in leaf-covered piles on the ground; the piles have to be turned three times, so the beans don't cook. When the pulp has disintegrated the beans are spread out to dry as we saw; again, they have to be turned constantly. An agent from Badou will collect them and sell them to the government marketing board. Cocoa was once a good crop, the farmer said, but prices fell drastically in the seventies and have only started to go up in the last year when there hasn't been enough rain. He was hoping the good "small rains" this September and October meant the drought was over.

While we were there, the farmer's wife and two of the older children were sitting on stools grating cassava into enamel basins on the ground. The grated cassava would be soaked, pressed to extract the starch (most of which is sold), fermented, and then roasted to make *gari*, which can be sprinkled dry over other food or cooked with water into a porridge. This was a fairly prosperous family; their compound had several buildings, and the children looked well nourished. But they grew almost everything they needed—even the palmettos to thatch the mud-brick buildings—and seemed to spend all their time doing so.

Throughout our visit, the farmer spoke Ewe, we spoke French, and Kayi interpreted between the two. When we got back to the car and he saw our guidebook, *Togo Today*, on the dashboard, he said, "Oh, you speak

English!" All along, we could have spoken English, as he had grown up and gone to school in "Togo Brittanique," the strip of German Togoland mandated to Britain as a result of World War I and now, since 1956, part of Ghana.

Leaving the cocoa plantation, we started looking for a picnic spot, but there was no place both open and shady. Finally the need for a bathroom drew us back to the hotel in Badou. When we asked if we could picnic on the grounds the staff invited us into the otherwise empty dining room and set us places over our protests that we didn't need to dirty dishes. We bought drinks all around and ate our bread and pâté in comfort. Travel in Togo is not hard, but it calls for unfamiliar strategies.

Monday

As usual, I'm finishing this up after lunch on Monday before going down to the Cultural Center to check the mail. This is my favorite time of day. The house is clean, Mahouna is gone, there's enough breeze, dead by late afternoon, to give the Japanese lampshade over the dining table a slight spin, and I'm not expected to be anywhere until three.

Sunday morning, we called on a Peace Corps volunteer Alidou had suggested we visit, a mechanic from Massachusetts, who kept his motorcycle in the living room and chickens in the bathroom. He directed us up rocky tracks on two sides of the basin to get views of the city from above. From above, through a fringe of slender teaks, Atakpamé looks most pleasant and picturesque. You understand why the Germans made it their administrative capital and forget how well the mellow-looking corrugated iron roofs conduct heat. We also drove east of town to the stone ruins of the old German governor's house, bombed during World War I. It's now full of millet from which a group of Kabyés camped out front were making beer.

When we took our guide home, he directed us to the Lomé road by a back way. Rounding a bend in the Sunday morning quiet, we came upon two men prancing about on stilts among the branches overhead. A few kids were watching them, and a couple of pedestrians were going about their business unimpressed. According to *Togo Today*, the stilt dance, or *chébé*, is local to the Atakpamé area and "is performed amid a mystical, religious atmosphere." Britt and Amy had seen it in the Sunday afternoon folklore show at the Hôtel Sarakawa (on one of their dates with Barbara and Beaugosse), but there, they said, the stilts were only about two feet tall. These guys, their legs tied to the stilts from ankle to knee, were at least ten feet off the ground. They adeptly caught coins we tossed and clowned in response. One of them squatted and kicked like a Russian folk dancer with twelve-foot calves. Perhaps the religious element is the faith these feats must take.

In Notsé, we stopped to buy squat, sweet little pineapples from one of the dozens of stands lining the road. This morning I gave one to Mahouna, who is from Notsé. He said, "Ah oui, the pineapples from Notsé are the real thing."

Neighbors
⊠ ⊠ ⊠ ⊠

My neighborhood is coming to life. Until classes started, I was the only one living in my block. Now three other apartments are occupied. And a few businesses—butcher, bakery, stationer's—have opened in the commercial center. The stationery store owners live in another section of the *cité*, I discovered on a walk. They told me that my section is almost all European because the houses are rented; their section is Togolese because the houses were sold and only Togolese allowed to buy.

My next-door neighbor is Vitaly, an exuberant Soviet-sponsored Russian professor. We meet out front every morning when the bread vendor comes by. He often tells me about his latest bargain in what seems to be a clothes-buying mission, but all he ever wears around home is a spandex bikini and rubber thongs. He's glad I speak English because I'll be someone for his wife to talk to. She's still in Leningrad making sure they get the better apartment they've been promised, but she's supposed to arrive by Christmas.

Next door to Vitaly is Régine, a French physics professor who has been here several years and isn't home much. I know her maid, Mathilde, better.

Early this month, Nick and Geeta moved in on the other side of Régine. He's a jazz musician from Boston; she's a graphic artist from Bombay. They met six months ago while Geeta was visiting her brother in Boston, fell in love, sold Nick's household stuff and most of Geeta's clothes and jewelry, and set off for India, via Togo so Nick could study Ewe drumming. When they arrived in Lomé, knowing no one, they went straight to the Indian shops and found rooms in an Indian merchant's house. But they gradually realized the merchant was cheating them and treating Geeta like a servant, so when a new Togolese friend helped them get this apartment, they were glad to move out on their own. Their furniture consists of a mattress on the floor, a few cushions and boxes, and a camp stove. They keep water and a few staples in Vitaly's refrigerator.

Geeta has shining hair and lively eyes, glides around in long scarlet and mustard skirts or pale Punjabi pajamas, and looks cool and graceful no matter what. Nick has long sandy hair and a beard, walks with a lope, looks clumsy and scruffy, and is absolutely high on being in Africa. He's already been taken to an all-night purification ceremony and made plans to go to a village where they make special bells. He'll eat and drink anything and invite home anyone who talks to him on the street. Geeta is outgoing and interested in Africa, too, but she boils their water and tells Nick not to trust everyone.

Alf and Edith Storey live in a villa along the path a couple of hundred yards behind the apartments. If I'm walking back from the pool at tea time, they halloo from their patio for me to join them. Visiting Alf and Edith has some of the appeal of watching television at the end of the day. Alf sits back, wearing a *pagne* and a tennis tan, like an off-duty colonial officer in Somerset Maugham, combs his fingers through the Clark Gable wave in his still-brown hair, and tells me what's wrong with the teaching of English at the university. He thinks the teaching of language is neglected in favor of literature; students should have to learn the language perfectly before studying literature. "You can't service an engine while it's running," he says.

Edith, a straightforward housewife, knows what's going on in the neighborhood: The former occupants of a villa near me moved out when they returned from their summer leave to find a family of green mambas in their bathtub. A neighboring houseboy who went crazy after a visit to his village said he'd been bewitched. The neighborhood bag lady, who sleeps in an empty garage and bathes in her clothes at an outside tap, was once a schoolteacher and still "marks" papers she finds in the garbage.

Alf and Edith have lived abroad, four or five years at a post, for the past twenty-five years. They're the old-timers among my friends in Togo, having been here four years. They seem to enjoy the role of surrogate parents—dispensers of tea, advice, background information, and household equipment—to younger and shorter-term Anglophones. But they're loners, too. Most of the people they befriend move on in a year or two. They feel betrayed by Callie and Trevor, who they think are using Britain's good name for private profit, and snubbed by their own children, who after an international upbringing settled down speedily to English suburban life. Alf is approaching retirement. Tired as he and Edith claim to be of

Third World conditions and transient relationships, they're apprehensive about settling in England, where their neighbors, they say, greet them with, "What, back are you? Where you been this time? Bloody hot there, eh?" and carry on about the football standings. They seem to need to find a place between England and abroad.

Although most of the people who live in this section of the *cité* are European, most of the people I see here are Togolese. The Europeans stay behind their walls; the Togolese hang out on the streets and paths. At noontime, schoolboys try to bat the clusters of small, soft, red, pear-shaped fruits they call *pommes* out of the tree in front of my dining room window. A neighboring houseboy shimmies up the coconut palms behind the apartment block to harvest coconuts. When he saw me watching him one quiet Sunday morning, he gave me two coconuts and showed me how to open them. Bare-breasted women with white *pagnes* around their waists— voodoo novices—gather palm fronds and coconut husks for fuel. University students pace the paths memorizing their lectures. Produce vendors trudge door to door under stacks of fruit-laden basins. Other women sit under the trees across from the pool selling snacks. Men with time on their hands sit on the curbs or stroll. And everyone stares at passersby.

It's unnerving to be stared at. I was contemptuous of the European women in the *cité* who drive the equivalent of a couple of blocks to the tennis courts, until I started taking tennis lessons myself and walking past the starers in shorts. The *cité* doesn't isolate foreigners from Togolese but from middle-class Togolese and thus exaggerates the economic and cultural gulf between Europeans and Africans.

There's a French family across the street that gets along without domestic servants, even though both parents teach, because they don't want their three children to grow up feeling that they should be waited upon. I often see the man taking out the garbage in the morning. He comes out in his shorts with a neatly tied plastic bag and deposits it in the basket on the street. As soon as he's back inside, scavengers appear, dump the garbage, pick through it, and take at least the bag. When part of a can of pâté had sat in my refrigerator too long to be trusted, I had to think about how to get rid of it. I could explain food poisoning to Mahouna and have him delay taking out the garbage until he saw the truck coming, or wait until Saturday and lie in wait for the garbage truck myself. In the end, I flushed the contents down the toilet.

After one week of tennis lessons, I realized that the soles of the old red

Nike running shoes I was wearing were too narrow for the sideways movements of tennis, so I went down to Bata and bought a pair of tennis shoes, white. After my next lesson, one of the ball boys followed me off the court repeating a request I couldn't understand. Finally the tennis teacher told me he was asking for "the old shoes."

One day as I approached the pool, I saw three ragged children lined up like stairsteps peering into the pool area through a gap in the shrubbery. The scene hit me like a photograph. I could see the fingers of six small hands curled through the wire fence, the sleeping baby sagging on the tallest girl's back, the bright bathing suits out of focus in the triangle over their heads. But it's a photograph I didn't get, because I was going swimming and didn't have my camera.

I'm writing this to the reverberation of masonry drills and banging iron. The Caisse is installing bars on the ground-floor windows of all the apartments to keep uninvited neighbors out. As far as I'm concerned, the Caisse is the intruder. The windows are so small and high I don't see how anyone could get in through them anyway, and the bars make the already dark bedroom feel like a prison cell.

"Avoir le Temps"
✉ ✉ ✉ ✉ ✉ ✉

Thursday morning, I breezed into the mimeo room in the EDL to pick up my copies of *Arms and the Man* for British lit and found the job only half done. They'd run out of paper, explained the mimeo operator, come back in two weeks. Oh well, I thought, the students can be reading the first couple of acts while I find a way to get the rest run off. Then I looked at the copies; she'd started from the end. So Friday morning, I took the remaining stencils back to the Cultural Center to ask Kay to beg Josèph to run them off there.

Then I went to the Sureté Nationale, for I think the seventh time, to pick up my *carte de séjour*. I applied for this identity card two months ago. It's not clear whether I need it—some sources say yes, some no. But I thought, when in doubt, be covered. I could see myself applying for an exit visa (yes, once in, you need permission to leave) and being asked where my *carte de séjour* was. And with local identification, I wouldn't have to carry my passport around. Every Friday since then, I've returned to pick it up and been told something further was required. First, I needed *timbres fiscales*, sold at the Service des Domaines a couple of blocks away. I couldn't just run over there, buy the stamps, and return, however, because the Service des Domaines was already closed for lunch. Then the letter of appointment from the American government was not enough to explain what I was doing in Togo, I needed one from the *directeur* of the Ecole des Lettres. Then I needed to supply not just five passport photos, but seven. (The pass for the pool at the *cité*, which no one ever looks at, required four.) Then I needed to return for "some inquiries," which turned out to be the statement that all was now in order except the fee. The embassy had told us specifically that foreigners working for Togolese institutions were exempt from the fee. I told the official that if I had to come back it would be with an officer of the American Embassy. Yesterday, Patrice, the Great Facilitator, went with me. We had to sit on a bench in the hall for some time while the official went out to breakfast, but I got my card without discussion. I think now that I was supposed to recognize most of the additional requirements as hints for "dash."

While we were waiting, Patrice observed, "C'est l'Afrique. On a le temps." I've heard this expression often. It could be used straight, with pride, as if to say, "There's no rush, we have time to talk and listen." But I've always heard it with some degree of edge. René said it with bemused tolerance when we were being forcibly entertained in his cousin's village. Patrice was clearly ironic. *He* didn't have the time. Back at his office, the phone was ringing, contractors were waiting, and the paperwork was piling up. And he may have suspected he was being intentionally inconvenienced. When one of the Sureté officers said something to another one in a local language, I asked Patrice what they were saying. He said, "I don't know; they're speaking Kabyé." Patrice is Ewe, a member of the southern elite that has had Western education and civil service preferment since colonial times. The Kabyé president has brought more northerners into the government, particularly the military and the police, and it's difficult to distinguish between affirmative action and ethnic nepotism.

Before I arrived in Togo, I envisioned myself spending days driving around the countryside, afternoons poking about in the market with my camera. Instead, I seem to spend my days chauffeuring paper up and down the Route d'Atakpamé and my afternoons visiting. Visiting makes me feel both that I "have the time" and that I don't. It's a nuisance when you're busy and want to make a five-minute phone call to have to allocate two hours during the approved visiting hours of four to six on a day when the people you want to talk to do not have, say, an English class at the Cultural Center and you yourself do not have a French lesson, to drive miles through puddles and over eroded railroad tracks, take your chances on finding them home, and if they are home, linger over refreshments and perhaps defer your message because they have other visitors, too. On the other hand, once you get there, it's a deep pleasure to sit on a patio over tea or beer and talk.

It's the intersection of African conditions and traditional values with European, or modern, institutions and expectations that can be frustrating. Nick told a story illustrating the problem the other day. He had agreed to talk about American music at the English conversation class at the Cultural Center at six o'clock on Wednesday. But his own drumming lesson has no fixed time. He goes to his teacher's house in the middle of the afternoon, and when the teacher is not rehearsing his group or entertaining visitors, Nick gets his lesson. This Wednesday, things went slowly, and Nick was caught between his African obligation to defer to the teacher's sense that "on a le temps" and his American obligation to show up on time.

Our Togolese colleagues are more seriously caught in this vise than Nick or I. One of the people I go to visit is Madame Abidji, a French teacher at the Lycée de Tokoin. We were introduced by the Cultural Center director, who knew that I wanted to improve my French and Madame Abidji wanted to learn English. The director, conscientious but not subtle in the performance of her duties, seized a moment when we both happened to be in the Cultural Center, shoved us together, and as much as said, "Now you can set times to meet, and speak French half the time and English the other half, and that way you'll both have free language lessons." Despite that introduction, we quickly became friends. On first meeting, most of my English Department colleagues seemed reserved, or anxious to demonstrate that they knew how deficient Togolese conditions would look to an American, or simply tongue-tied. But Madame Abidji was warm and open and assumed we had things in common. She wants to know everything about the U.S. because her husband, a history professor, is there now working on a Ph.D. She hopes to get a fellowship herself and join him by the end of this year, which is why she was looking for an English teacher. But she doesn't want to speak English with me; she says she isn't ready for conversation, she needs structured lessons. So I get all the language profit from our conversations.

Every two or three weeks, I drive up to her house in Agouenyivé, a village about five miles north of the university, a little after four. As soon as I turn off the Route d'Atakpamé and cross the railroad tracks, I'm in another world, where cars are a novelty. Children run after the car singing "Yovo, yovo, Bonsoir." I pass a fetish on the right, a figure like a fat beaver under a grass shelter, and a little farther, on the left, the Bar Moderne, where a rubber-legged couple holding martini glasses jitterbugs on the wall.

Madame Abidji sends the teenage cousin who provides live-in help to this same bar for beer and bubblegum soda, and we sit on the porch and talk. Her two girls, six and eight, decline the soda and play quietly in the farthest corner of the yard; three-year-old Kodjogan clambers over his mother, teases for more soda, and spills it on her. We compare life in Togo and the U.S. and ask each other naive questions. Whenever either of us suddenly understands the other's point, or Madame Abidji wants to express emphatic agreement, she says, "aanh-HHAANH!" This is a typical Togolese verbal gesture, but she puts her whole self into it. Her French is so clear and her attention so sympathetic that I suddenly become fluent when I'm with her.

If she wants structured English lessons, why doesn't she take an evening course at the American Cultural Center? Because, with her husband away, she's the single parent of three young children, and Agouenyivé, which will one day be a suburb of Lomé, is now complexly inconvenient. Her husband is away to get the Ph.D. that will allow him to keep his post at the university. They built a house in Agouenyivé because that's where they could afford land and they knew that it would eventually have city services. In the meantime, however, they have no electricity, which means that they have no way to pump water from their well into the pipes in the house, which makes every washing operation laborious, and no refrigeration, so Madame Abidji has to shop frequently. Getting to Lomé is an hour-long production and a significant expense. She has to walk about a mile on a dirt track to get to the taxi park on the Route d'Atakpamé, then wait till a taxi going to Lomé fills up. On the way back, the taxi driver may take her all the way home, but most drivers refuse to drive over the eroded railroad tracks, which could peel the bottom off a gas tank. She has to leave home before six in the morning to get to school on time and often go to the *marché* before returning in the afternoon. Even so, she's lucky because all her classes are in the morning. If she had to return after the long lunch break, she'd be in town till after six, because it would be too hard and expensive to get home and back between twelve and three. She has the teenage cousin to do the heavy work and look after the children when she's not there, but it's not a life that permits going out in the evening. My contribution to the reciprocal arrangement envisioned by the Cultural Center director is not to speak English with Madame Abidji but to take her to the receptions and dinners (Thanksgiving this week) that the director invites her to.

Yesterday I invited the English Department for drinks at six. Those who came, about half the department, seemed to think it was novel—and nice—to get together with colleagues for drinks on a Friday afternoon. Everyone but Alf Storey, Madame Yamajako (the French wife of a Togolese judge), and me has a second job and an extended family. Over-scheduled as I sometimes feel, we're the ones with time.

Birthday
☒ ☒ ☒

Yesterday René appeared at the door with a birthday cake. He thrust the cake box into my hands, kissed me on both cheeks, said, "Happy birthday," and fled. He was gone before I remembered we'd discovered we had a mutual birthday at Callie and Trevor's dinner party back in September. I had no time either to wish him a happy birthday, too, or to tell him off. What I wished I'd done, a moment later, is shoved the cake back at him. I took it to the Cultural Center and passed it around to the staff.

Why did he do this? Pity? Guilt? A few weeks ago I thought, well, he wasn't my type anyway, I was interested in him as a colleague rather than a lover, so much the better that he had another girlfriend, perhaps we could still be friends. But he wasn't interested. He was always gracious when we ran into each other, but never had time to talk. Instead, he makes a gesture that tricks me into saying thank you and prevents me from saying anything else. Exactly what bothered me from the beginning: control through perfect manners.

If he was never my type, why am I so angry? Maybe that's part of the reason. He pushed me to violate my own personality and then rejected the sacrifice. Of course, it wasn't only he that influenced me, but the situation. I wanted to visit the village and go to the labor history seminar, and what I thought I'd lost when he left was not so much him as a means of getting acquainted with the society. How else to become intimate with the society if not to become intimate with people? But to do so do you have to become the person they want you to be?

Maybe from his point of view I was using him as a tour guide. But that's what he offered from the first date when he took me to L'Abreuvoir to watch the prostitutes before going to Le Chess to dance. L'Abreuvoir for voyeurism, Le Chess where the international class shows off, La Cachette with Philippe—none of my experiences of Lomé nightclubs has been simple.

Did he represent himself as interested in travel and photography in order to impress me? Did I allow myself to accept him because I was interested in travel? Was I using him for cultural experience? Was he using my interest in the culture as a means of seduction? Was he interested in me or in a white woman?

I've learned he has a reputation for trying out all the unattached white women who come through town, which makes me glad we didn't last long enough for me to get known as "René's girlfriend," but it also makes me wonder about what life is like for him beneath the French silk shirts and gallantry. What does it mean for his sense of self if he seeks out partners for whom he is part of an experimental and temporary experience of another culture? I think of the story he told at the Lloyds' of being stood up by American friends on Christmas. Does he seek out people who have no choice but to betray him—in the end by going home, but from the beginning by relating to him in a way conditioned by temporariness and cultural difference? Which comes back to the original question: Can an outsider have genuine relationships here without renouncing all the things that make one an outsider, starting with the departure date?

I had a very pleasant outsiders' evening out with Kay—dinner at Le Basilic, where every dish contains basil, and a slide show at the French Cultural Center about a boat trip on the Niger River. Kay takes the true friend's rather tricky position on René, whom she knew and liked before I arrived: It's no wonder I fell for him because he's very attractive and no wonder I'm furious because he's proved a perfect cad.

New Clothes
✉ ✉ ✉ ✉ ✉

The hotter it gets the less I have to wear. The clothes I brought are all too hot; they're 100 percent cotton, but they have sleeves and waistbands.

At first I bought market dresses. One day Lee Ann and I met for lunch at the Café de l'Amitié, a little Malian restaurant in the market, and then made a tour of the Senegalese dress vendors nearby. I learned that noon, when the streets are empty and the vendors half asleep, is the time to go to the market, and that bargaining is not the formidable competition I'd imagined, but a sociable game. Lee Ann introduced me to her boubou vendor. Much was made of the fact that Lee Ann was a *bon client* and I was ready to become one. The vendor asked if I were "Corps de la Paix," which would have been a point in my favor. By the time we'd discussed the virtues of 100 percent cotton and our common experience of being foreigners, however, I got my two dresses—a green boubou with white pineapples stenciled around the hem and a dress-length dashiki in indigo tie-dye—for 2,000 francs apiece, which Lee Ann pronounced a good price.

I wore the indigo the next day and was so busy with errands and appointments that I didn't discover till I got home around five that I'd turned blue: blue neck, blue arms, blue underwear, blue-streaked face, and deep indigo armpits and fingernails that retained their cast for a week. "Oh yes," said Mahouna the next morning, "you have to soak dyed clothes in cold salt water to set the dye," information he could have imparted before I left for the day in the new dress. These dresses have now been soaked and washed several times, and they still leave a tinge. Now I'm trying a dressmaker.

I borrowed a Vogue pattern book from Callie Lloyd and traced the pictures of the styles I liked. "I prefer European clothes, don't you?" said Callie when I asked for the book; "I think they're more smart." I have to agree, though I wish it weren't with her. Vera took me to the Lebanese fabric shops she prefers and then to her European dressmaker, Josephine. Josephine herself isn't European; she's the one Vera goes to for her European clothes. Vera has another dressmaker for her African *complets*.

Josephine lives in the first two-story house on the right on a typical residential obstacle course of holes, garbage piles, and chickens. Inside her wall, some stage of meal preparation is always in progress. In the late afternoon, the time I usually go there, a young man stands in front of a portable blackboard teaching arithmetic to half a dozen children seated on the ground. For a fitting, an old woman who doesn't speak French takes me into a room full of broken-down furniture, closes the shutters for privacy from the children in the yard, and tugs and pins the dress to her satisfaction.

The first time I went to Josephine, I gave her a picture of the dress I wanted and the fabric, she took my measurements, and three days later the dress was done and perfect. I was so pleased I took her some more material—this time batik from the workshop for the handicapped—and asked her to make another just like it. The second dress took five trips because it wasn't ready to be tried on or picked up when promised, and its proportions turned out a little different from the one I liked. I seem to have become a *bon client*.

The best-dressed students, Alidou tells me, buy all their clothes at the "dead *yovo*" market in the Grand Marché, a block-long rummage sale of the clothes Europeans and Americans give to charity. I break into a sweat just looking at jeans, knit shirts, and polyester dresses. It's called the "dead *yovo*" market because who but a dead person could afford to give away such good clothes?

Information

⊠ ⊠ ⊠ ⊠

What do I miss in Togo? Lomé is a free port, so there's no consumer item you can get in France that you can't get here. It's true that SGGG doesn't carry cottage cheese and that only one bakery makes whole-grain bread, but the compensations in Camembert, papayas, and duty-free liquor make the expatriate consumer's lot anything but hard.

What I miss is information—from what's playing at the movies to what's happening in the world. One day at the end of October, I ran into Philippe downtown, and he asked, "Did you hear the United States invaded Grenada?"

"What! Ce n'est pas possible! The United States doesn't go around invading little islands." Ten days later, when the international edition of *Newsweek* arrived, I got to read all about it. Or rather, not all, and that's the problem. The Togolese government censors anything "subversive," and the Cultural Center library offers nothing more skeptical than *Newsweek*.

At first, just getting access to the information available was a challenge. The local (that is, only) newspaper, such as it is, is not delivered and not sold along with the Marlboros and chewing sticks at neighborhood stands; you have to go downtown to a bookstore to get it. The paper prints a movie schedule, but only for the current day, and the movies play musical chairs among the various theaters and show times, so if you want to plan ahead, you have to pick up a weekly schedule at a theater, which means you have to go to the movies Saturday night when the schedule comes out because by Sunday it will be gone.

So it seemed like the sudden dawn of rationality when the stationery store opened in the commercial center a few weeks ago. Now I get the Togolese paper most days and have a standing order for the *International Herald Tribune*. Yesterday they even had a stack of movie schedules. The

Trib arrives once a week, on Wednesdays. There are supposed to be six issues, but I haven't received more than four or five. The proprietor blames the missing issues on the censor. Whether the missing issues contain something the government considers subversive, or some are withheld on principle, or the censor is overloaded, I don't know.

The Togolese newspaper, radio station, television station, and monthly magazine are all run by the same government agency. The lead story in *La Nouvelle Marche* ("the new initiative") is always the daily schedule of the president, who is always referred to on first reference, with a verbal trumpet roll, as "le président-fondateur du RPT, président de la République, le général Gnassingbé Eyadéma," and on second reference as "l'homme du treize janvier," which is National Liberation Day, the anniversary not of independence from France but of the 1967 coup that brought Eyadéma to power. Eyadéma's recent visit to the United States was a gold mine the paper worked for all it was worth. The reportage was cumulative, like "Old MacDonald's Farm." Each day's story told the most recent events and repeated each previous day's report. My favorite headline appeared the following week: "After the success of his official visit to the USA, President Eyadéma received Thursday a warm welcome from the people of Kozah and Doufelgou."

The rest of the domestic news consists of reports of development projects (all successful) and training seminars for workers (like the one for English teachers coming up in Atakpamé). Selected international news is picked up from Reuters and Agence-France-Press. The selection includes bombings in Lebanon and developments in the anti-apartheid movement, ignores international criticism of Marcos and Duvalier. There's a page each of news in Ewe and Kabyé, the designated national languages, a page of obituaries, and a page of sports. Every Wednesday, there's a women's page with a recipe and articles about things like telephone manners and puberty. The radio repeats the newspaper; the TV adds some news photography from French television; the magazine retells the success stories of the month.

The official version of Togolese history is contained in a superhero comic book called *Once Upon a Time There Was . . . EYADEMA.* (Peace Corps volunteers call Eyadéma, whose first name was Etienne before he decreed that all Togolese must have African names, "Stevie Wonder.") The story opens with the birth of little Eyadéma in the pastoral Kabyé village of Pya, north of Lama Kara. His farmer father is soon killed resisting a brutal French foreman while working as conscript labor on a road. The fatherless boy excels at school, sports, and hunting and is polite to his elders. Elders and peers alike recognize him as a leader. At fifteen, he gives up his books, "with rage in his heart," to "take up the hoe of his fathers." But conscription into the French army allows him to expand his horizons. He rises rapidly in rank and the estimation of his officers, at the same time questioning the French action, in which he is participating, against nationalist movements in Indochina and Algeria.

While Eyadéma is abroad, unrest in Togo leads to independence (in 1960); when he returns home the ethnically biased head of state, Sylvanus Olympio, a southerner, is excluding northerners from national life. "Because Olympio practices authoritarianism, the crisis cannot be solved except through violence," intones the narrator. Eyadéma sees that "to refuse to act would be treason" and in 1963 leads a coup that kills Olympio. His colleagues urge him to take power, but he says, "No, the army does not belong in politics, its place is in the barracks." The opposition leader, Nicolas Grunitzky, is installed as president and appoints a northerner as vice-president. Before long, however, the unity of this government collapses, and in 1967 Eyadéma is once more forced to intervene. This time the coup takes place "without spilling a drop of blood," apparently in a cabinet meeting.

From here on, Colonel Eyadéma keeps trying to withdraw from power and the people keep insisting he stay. He mixes fearlessly with the people in the markets and on the playing fields. He walks away unscathed from an assassination attempt and a suspicious plane crash, and the people proclaim "a miracle!" In 1969, he establishes the Rassemblement du Peuple Togolais (RPT), "not a party, but a single and veritable national melting pot," to give the people a voice and a structure for choosing their own leader. When election time comes in 1972, only at the unanimous insistence of the Togolese people, and "in the greater interest of the nation," does Eyadéma agree to be a candidate. His election, by 99.87 percent of the electorate, allows him to undertake the battle for the economic independence of the country, which consists principally in nationalizing the phosphate industry, building the port and the north-south road, and joining ECOWAS.

The result of this history of humble and high-minded deference to the will of the people is whispers. Togo is a small country. Everybody knows somebody who is in prison or died in prison. But the references are oblique. My colleagues and the students who talk to me after class all say you've got to assume an informer in every class.

Still, in the absence of other information, the myth is strong. When I asked Alidou—holder of a *maîtrise* in law—about some point in Togolese history, he said, "You've got the history of Togo right there in the bookcase, let's look it up." He meant the comic book.

Integrated Development

⊠ ⊠ ⊠ ⊠ ⊠ ⊠ ⊠ ⊠

Last Sunday afternoon, two sunburned men appeared at my door to ask if I wanted to go with them to the Sio River Integrated Development Project this week. It took me a minute to grasp that they were the directors of the project the AID program director had said I might be able to visit as a photographer. I'd forgotten how desperate I was a month ago to get out of Lomé and do something that made me feel connected.

We met for lunch today at Keur Rama, then drove in their Land Cruiser to a district between the Atakpamé and Kpalimé roads. It's only about thirty kilometers from Lomé, but I would never have found it or attempted the road in my car. Once we left the Route d'Atakpamé at Agouenyivé we were bounced around so hard in the vehicle that conversation stopped and I thought about the merits of a pith helmet. The only traffic we saw for fifteen kilometers was a bicycle and, on an intersecting path through the hip-high grass, a stately line of women carrying huge clay water jars on their heads.

Jon and Larry work for one of the many not-for-profit development organizations that propose and implement the projects USAID funds. The Sio River project is now in a one-year pilot stage to test its hypotheses before long-term funding is approved. The idea is to improve the economy of the region by assisting all its productive activities, small businesses as well as agriculture. In the 1960s and 1970s, first Taiwan and then the People's Republic of China built an irrigation system and taught farmers to grow rice. The dam and canal system are still in good shape, but since the Chinese left in 1979, most of the irrigated land has lain idle, and what's been cultivated has produced only half what it could. The problem, said Jon, the project social scientist, is that a development plan based on rice culture didn't take into account the way people actually lived. It required them to devote a lot of labor to transplanting rice, which they consider a cash crop, at the same time they needed to be planting and hoeing corn, their major food crop. And it ignored other economic activities like livestock raising, crafts, and trade. The goal of this project is to improve the productivity of the activities the people already pursue rather than to change the activities.

One of its hypotheses is that not all farmers want to grow rice. They may not have enough family labor to grow rice in addition to food crops, or they may earn enough cash from other activities. So the project includes experiments with growing corn within the irrigated area originally reserved for rice. Another hypothesis is that farmers might be more willing to grow rice if it didn't require so much labor, so the project also includes experiments with broadcasting instead of transplanting rice. A third hypothesis is that people often can't start or expand economic activities because they don't have access to credit, so it provides loans (and training in how to repay them) to both farmers and small businesses.

We stopped first at several agricultural sites. I took pictures of transplanted rice and broadcast rice, well-spaced rice and ill-spaced rice, healthy corn growing up the sides of the levee and weeds in a low field where the corn had drowned. Lots of little details revealed the economic and agricultural realities. On the concrete in front of the agricultural extension station garage in Mission Tové, a row of rusty red Chinese tractor carcasses faced a carpet of bright red peppers drying in the sun. As we walked on a levee between irrigated cornfields, Larry, the agronomist, pointed out that the low plants growing on top of the levee weren't weeds, but okra; people were making use of every bit of fertile land. Labor is so cheap that in a successful farmer's field human scarecrows waved their arms.

In the village of Koviépé, where we visited a restaurant and a weaver's workshop that had received loans, almost everybody was either off in the fields or asleep. Under a tree in the square, a man and woman sat behind two tables spread with matches, bouillon cubes, wrapped candy in mayonnaise jars, peanuts in what looked like cough-syrup bottles (aspirin, Jon said, they use a lot of it), and glass-sided boxes of fried cakes and *gari*. Two men straddling a bench looked up from a game of *warri* balanced between them on their knees. A blackboard hanging on a grass house at the edge of the square announced the day's lottery results. A chalked message on a closed wooden shutter proclaimed what could be taken as antidevelopment philosophy: "Le grand problème de l'homme est l'homme."

The restaurant owner stood behind three enamel basins covered with cloths ready to serve invisible customers. She proudly showed me the rest of her establishment—the small, dark dining room with a low wooden table and two benches on the dirt floor, and the kitchen, where a blackened pot held up by stones sat on a fire dangerously close to the smoke-blackened rush wall.

The weaver and his friend leaned on the outside wall of his shop watching two boys operate the narrow local looms. Mustard and white silk warp yarns stretched far out into the square, held in place by rocks. The weaver had used his loan to hire these apprentices and buy more yarn. The appeal of, and hence market for, his weaving is limited by the variety of colors he can offer. This is limited by the amount of yarn he can afford to stock, in which the loan assisted, but also by the colors available. I realized this as it became clear that my role was not only photographer but customer. I was supposed to order something based on the colors and designs the weaver was showing me. I didn't mind, because I want to buy some local weaving and it doesn't get any more local than this, but the colors he had all struck me as either dull or garish. In the end, I asked for a mauve-and-loden-striped *pagne* like one he had already made. It's not striking, but it is characteristic. On the way home, we passed a man on a bicycle wrapped in just such a cloth.

While I tried to make up my mind, the weaver and his buddy bantered with Jon. When was he going to grow out of short pants, they wanted to know, referring to his madras Bermudas. He bantered back in easy African-French vernacular. It's no wonder he seemed at home there, Larry told me. He's lived in Africa ever since he was a Peace Corps volunteer twenty years ago. When he goes home now it's to his Zairian wife and four children in a village outside Ouagadougou.

Over a beer at my house afterward, Jon explained his approach to development: "We go into a bar and have a beer and just casually ask, 'Where's the hard-boiled eggs?' And a couple of weeks later we go back, and there's a plate of hard-boiled eggs."

I'd been thinking that to be comfortable in Togo, you have to be either impervious to Africa, like Callie and Trevor, or totally committed, like Jon. You can't straddle the gap between worlds as I'm trying to do. And yet, Jon straddles too. His wife and children and permanent address are African, but he has an American salary, and he doesn't let African men tease him out of wearing Bermudas. He's one of the guys in the bar, but he has the distance to mention hard-boiled eggs. There's just such a fine line between his worlds.

1984

⊠ ⊠

The day the EDL ran out of paper after copying the back half of *Arms and the Man* I knew I had to have a book for British lit next semester. The students can afford one paperback; a single book is the standard reading for a course here; and Trevor Lloyd offered to include my order in his monthly air-freight shipment for the British School. But it would have to be a many-faceted book for me to stand to deal with it for a whole semester, and I had to choose it by Thursday, when Trevor needed the order.

When I saw *Time*'s cover story on George Orwell, it occurred to me that *1984* was British, modern, multifaceted, relevant, and, for a term that begins in February 1984, timely. The trouble is that the relevance of this choice is also its liability. The features of totalitarian Oceania are all too familiar here. Dissenters disappear; history is rewritten; slogans have an independent life (on my recently acquired *carte de séjour*, "Travail-Liberté-Paix" has been xxxx'd out with a typewriter and replaced with "Union-Paix-Solidarité"); there's even a party uniform (a safari suit with a portrait of Eyadéma pinned to the pocket). The concept of Big Brother is just a brilliant conflation of the portrait of "Number One" surveying every public room and the spiderweb of spies. What happened to Winston Smith could happen in my classroom.

I found a copy of the novel in the university library (part of the collection the British Council donated to the university when it left Lomé) and stayed up one night rereading it. Then I asked several colleagues whether they thought I could teach it.

Koami Johnson said, "Do it, do it. Somebody has to do it, and better you than we."

Alf Storey said, "That's a good way to cause yourself a lot of bother."

The Cultural Center director, in effect my boss, said, "So you want to become persona non grata?"

101

In the end, I thought of the potential for misunderstanding in a class of sixty students with imperfect English, the written exams subject to outside scrutiny, and the prospect of being stuck for a whole semester with no exit if it didn't work out, and did what (I say) any Togolese professor would have done, ordered a collection of short stories. I don't know, though, whether I was being prudent or timid. It's hard to imagine anyone being organized enough to read all those exams.

I'm beginning to feel like part of the English Department. Thursday evening we had an emergency meeting in which, to my surprise, the department stood up to the administration, which has decreed that, for TEFL classes, an hour of class will count for only half an hour of teaching credit. Since TEFL classes are a big part of the department's load, this is a way for the administration to solve the staff shortage by making the faculty work overtime without pay. Dagadou was ready to capitulate, but the other department members toughened him up. The conclusion is that a delegation is going to protest to the *directeur* of the EDL and then, because they know he won't do anything, to the *recteur* of the university.

It was interesting how the other department members dealt with Dagadou. They all thought he was failing his responsibility to represent their interests, but no one attacked him. Instead they gave him the support he needed to do what he ought to do. When I remarked on this to Elise afterward, she said the department headship rotates every three years. Koami had it before; she'll probably have it next. Everyone knows Dagadou is weak, but he's one of them, so they stand by him; and he's the head, so they give him respect.

Last night I saw another side of Dagadou, and of university politics, at a dinner party at Koami Johnson's. This is the first invitation I've had from any colleague besides Elise. The Dagadous, Elise, and a nonuniversity friend of Koami's were there. We sat around a low table on the terrace, drank a lot of wine, and talked like old friends suddenly ungagged: Conrad's politics, Jesse Jackson, the experience of foreign wives in Togo (Madame Johnson is French, Madame Dagadou Bahamian), comparative grad schools, beers, Catholicism, and Cultural Center directors. Koami grilled brochettes; Miles and Monk competed with African pop from the bar across the street; the Johnson children wandered out every so often for attention. Dagadou, who seems so unequal to departmental decisions, was an ironic step ahead in conversation. By two A.M., he and I were joining forces to get Koami to let us go home while we could still drive. After the

Cultural Center director's stiff parties with education bureaucrats who wear Eyadéma pins and leave promptly at 10:15, this evening was so normal it was overwhelming.

Madame Johnson said it was an extraordinary event for them, too. Until recently, they felt that social gatherings of professors were suspect as conspiracy. The lack of space for faculty members to hang out in the EDL is only partly economic.

Koami and Dagadou are urging me to stay a second year. Koami is talking about our team-teaching a course on Conrad and starting a *maîtrise* in American literature. There will be a new Cultural Center director and English teaching officer next year; he and Dagadou think that I, an old hand by then, could influence them to listen to university faculty instead of just Ministry of Education bureaucrats. This is flattering but doubtful. Still, they made me think about staying on. If we really could work together, it could be exciting.

Roommates
✉ ✉ ✉ ✉

Elise and I drove up to Atakpamé together for the English teachers' in-service seminar and shared a room.

As a woman and someone with an American education, Elise is the colleague I have the most in common with; and in these particular ways, she has more in common with me than with other colleagues. We've been to each other's houses and know each other's phone numbers. You'd think that sharing a room at a conference would be all it would take to make us confidential.

But it didn't work out that way. We'd been told that single rooms had been reserved for us, but when we arrived, the desk clerk had only a twin. Even though we both preferred to share (Elise to save money and I for the company), there was an awkward moment at the desk when neither of us was sure the other was willing. In a way, we're too much alike—both too reserved to volunteer intimacies and too respectful of the other's privacy to pry. In another way, our being together emphasized the differences more than the commonalities in our circumstances. I canceled my Wednesday morning class without a thought so we would get to Atakpamé in plenty of time for our afternoon lectures; she had to get permission to cancel hers. We shared a room, but she was the only Togolese in the hotel; the teachers stayed in the spartan dorms at the Ecole Normale.

Because she spent nine years in the U.S., I tend not to make the cultural adjustments when talking with Elise that I do with most other people. I figure she'll know what I mean. But I keep being surprised at how differently we understand things. When she invited me to lunch at her house, I was uncomfortable because she didn't introduce the children and though she chided them for speaking Mina, which I didn't understand, she continued to speak English with me, which they didn't understand. It seemed to me wrong to exclude the children and awkward not to let a guest know who was who. I knew that only two of the six children I saw were hers, but not which two or why only two of the others sat at the table with us and two stayed out in the yard.

Another time, I invited her to a play at the RPT building. When we parked the car, a whole gang of boys came up to "guard" it. Usually, I pick out one, offer a price, and, if he's still there when I return, pay him. But Elise, perhaps embarrassed by extortionist-beggars in my company, said, "The police ought to chase those boys away," and so I, not wanting to contribute to what she considered a public nuisance, ignored them. When we came out, not having contracted to pay the one who remained, I didn't. But *she* gave him something, saying, "Maybe he can buy some bread tonight." And I felt like a complete *yovo*.

Christmas
✉ ✉ ✉ ✉

The Atakpamé seminar was timed badly for the Togolese teachers, but perfectly for me. It meant that I didn't think about Christmas till the doorbell woke me up on Christmas Eve morning. It was Vitaly's occasional housekeeper delivering a gift packet of postcards of Leningrad. Over breakfast I decided to invite Vitaly, Nick, and Geeta to dinner. They were all home when I went around to invite them and all free for dinner.

I spent most of the day in the market with Kay's cousin Roger, who's visiting here for several weeks. The market had a special Christmas energy—a brisk business in chickens and ducks; seasonal stands playing Bach chorales to attract attention to their made-in-China tinsel and *yovo* dolls; an easy atmosphere, as though this day the business of buying and selling was rather a game. We ran into a teenage boy trying to sell two aquaria he'd made himself, squat corked bottles filled with sand, water, plants, and tiny fish. In contrast to all the food, soap, watches, and fake hair, even the tinsel, they were so useless and imaginative I bought one for Britt and Amy.

My dinner preparations consisted of bringing a papaya home from the market, walking over to the Commercial Center for one of the butcher's Provençal-herb-stuffed roasted chickens, boiling potatoes in their skins, making a salad, taking a cake out of the freezer. We had a lovely time. Vitaly is a movie fanatic, which gives him lots of material for stories. First, the plots of many films, none of them bad. Second, his adventures trying to get home from the movies at night without a car, which lead naturally into his vexed relations with his own embassy compatriots, who won't give him a ride even when they're going in the same direction without charging taxi fare. Nick regaled us with innocent-abroad tales of the *yovo* in the African drumming troupe. With the help of a little wine, Vitaly who doesn't speak English, and Nick, who barely speaks French, understood each other fine.

Yesterday, after breakfast here and a leisurely morning swimming at the Sarakawa, Britt and Amy and I went to Christmas dinner at Kay's. This was a strictly unofficial party; no one was there to represent anything. Everyone was either a friend of Kay's or a stranger, but we were all related by being cut off from the usual social supports. Besides the students and singles, there were Vera and Philippe, who are geographically distant from her family and emotionally distant from his; Monette Dablaka, the new Quebecoise secretary at the Cultural Center, and her Togolese husband and three-year-old son, who have just moved to Togo from Canada; and two Peace Corps volunteers from Upper Volta vacationing in Lomé, where they know no one. Clarence, specially engaged for the day, had made a fine turkey dinner; Kay had stuck a bunch of filao branches in a flowerpot to serve as a tree; Kevin Bennert, the consul, brought his guitar; everyone contributed something to the sense of festivity. After dark, we all gathered in the air-conditioned living room and sang carols, which made Monette homesick (I'd never noticed how many carols refer to snow). Eventually, we put on a tape of the *Messiah* and sang along, more or less in parts, to the "Hallelujah Chorus."

Britt and Amy had been apprehensive about Christmas away from home, but they agreed this was a lovely one—festivity and friendship without fuss. I didn't realize what a burden the usual Christmas gift- and party-giving routine is until I was free of it. One of the reasons we appreciated Kay's filao-branch Christmas tree is that it wasn't the real thing. In a way we were celebrating expatriate life, the chance to consider if not quite choose attachments while detached from home.

Tomorrow I'm going to Benin for two days with Julie Assani, one of the teachers on the Atakpamé seminar-planning committee.

1984

Tourists in Benin

⊠ ⊠ ⊠ ⊠ ⊠ ⊠

Julie and I made a good team on our trip to Benin. I provided the idea and the car. She provided wonderful relatives in Cotonou and invaluable local know-how—for example, which of several unmarked lines to stand in first at the border and how to chat up the officials. Julie's in her late twenties and has been teaching for four years since graduating from the university. As a single professional, she has unusual personal and financial freedom, but also a kind of mental freedom, a sense of adventure and possibility.

Unlike Togo, Benin has developed tourist sites, partly because it has "history" in a way that Togo doesn't. Togo is a settlement of refugees from the slave raiding that sustained the kingdom of Dahomey and financed the palace in Abomey and the colonial port of Ouidah that are now the principal things to see.

We stopped before lunch in Ouidah, now a sleepy town of sand streets and crumbling houses. The sights are a museum in the old Portuguese fort, the temple of the sacred python, and the house of Francisco de Souza, the Brazilian slave trader who helped King Ghézo seize the throne from his brother in 1818 and was rewarded with an official position in the king's court. I've been reading about him in Bruce Chatwin's novel *The Viceroy of Ouidah*. The museum was not much. The guide, napping under a tree when we arrived, led us through a miscellaneous collection of decaying pictures and artifacts of voodoo and the slave trade, pointing out *"esclaves"* and "tam-tams." The temple of the sacred python was a gyp. One of about a dozen women sleeping in the entrance took us to a cage inside the compound and picked up a small knotted-up snake. A man who spoke some French came out and gave one-word answers to our questions. We gave him 500 francs "for the temple." He extorted another 500 "for the guide." De Souza's house we never found. We'd ask someone where it was, and he'd say

111

that way; we'd go that way and ask again, and the next person would direct us back where we came from.

Ganvié, a village built on stilts in the lagoon just north of Cotonou, was a different story. It's appealingly picturesque, the motif of a lot of local art, including a picture I found hanging in my apartment, and highly developed. Julie remembers going there as a child when you negotiated with a fisherman to take you out to the village in a pirogue. Now the state tourist board has taken over. There's a restaurant on shore called La Pirogue, with a parking lot for tour buses, and you go out to the village in a motor launch for the hefty price of 3,000 francs. We arrived just after a big tour group had taken all the boats, so we had awhile to poke around the shore area. Across the water from the dock was a little market where pirogues were parked in front of the stalls and pigs wallowed in the shallows. Pirogues came in from the lagoon with loads of fish and went out with crates of Fanta and beer. With the help of the motor-launch ticket seller, Julie bought some fish from a woman in a pirogue to take to her cousins in Cotonou. She needed help because she didn't speak the local language and the woman didn't speak French. It startled her a little to be unable to communicate so close to home.

A thirteen-year-old boy adopted us and asked for a pen. He told us that the bundles of leafy sticks we saw piled up on the shore would be planted leaf-end down in circles in the lagoon, which is only about three feet deep. As the leaves decomposed, fish would come to feed on them; then men would catch the fish in nets. He also told us he didn't go to school, because his father didn't think school was necessary for a fisherman. We asked where he'd learned his quite good French; he'd picked it up from his older brother, who had worked in Gabon. We gave him the pen.

On the way out to the village, boys in pirogues, their round, silver paddle blades flashing in the sunlight, raced to draft in the boat's wake. Fishermen flung their nets in diaphanous arcs. On the way back, the low sun turned the water silver and shone through the holes in a silhouetted sail. The houses of wattle with hip roofs of thatch gave the village a Polynesian look. Signs on some of them identified a tailor, a general store, a restaurant, the post office. We passed the bakery pirogue, bristling with baguettes; a flock of pirogues, each with a line of jerry cans, waited at the fresh-water spring. All very picturesque.

But pathetic, too. The *toilettes* in the house we went into—a souvenir shop, naturally—were simply holes over the water the people fished and bathed in. Children waved to us from the verandas, but the adults looked distinctly displeased to be gawked at and photographed. The village was established, the guide said, by people fleeing the Fon slave raiders, who were afraid of water. Later their situation on the lagoon helped them evade the French tax collector. But now they're paying. The government is making money off their picturesqueness, and since they've lost the informal pirogue-taxi business, they're getting nothing.

As soon as we'd found a hotel in Cotonou, we went to Julie's cousin's house and presented her with the fish (kept fresh in the cooler by frozen bottles of drinking water). Dagigi and her husband, Sylvan, and their six children welcomed us without surprise though they hadn't known we were coming. Julie visits them often, always without warning; they're always home and always glad to see her. One reason they're always home is that it's difficult for government employees—he's a teacher and she's a secretary in a government office—to get permits to leave the country, and the only place they'd want to go is Lomé, where they have relatives. Teachers in Togo have a similar problem; Julie keeps her student ID to facilitate travel.

Although we'd dropped in unannounced on a two-career family with six kids on a weeknight, they acted as if they had nothing else to do. Sylvan brought chairs out to the cement yard between the kitchen and the house so we could visit while Dagigi cooked. She sat over the coalpot stirring and tasting like a priest conjuring spirits from the smoke. One of the children fanned the fire, and Sylvan, Julie, and I compared life in Cotonou and Lomé. Food is cheaper in Cotonou, we determined, but luxuries are more expensive. The roads in Cotonou are worse than in Lomé, and I find the general aspect visually grim—a combination of cement and decay—in contrast to Lomé's light open air.

When dinner was ready, the adults ate at a low table in the fluorescent-lit living room. One of the daughters brought in a basin of water and box of soap powder for hand washing; Sylvan opened bottles of orange and pineapple soda. The sauce was delicious, a mysterious transformation of everyday fish, tomatoes, onions, and peppers into ambrosia. So I was surprised as I finished my plate that Julie asked if I hadn't liked it. It turns out that leaving the fish heads is a *faux pas*; they're the best part. But no one seemed to mind when I offered them to Julie. Dagigi and Sylvan invited me back when I return to Cotonou to lecture in February. I took a lot of family pictures, which should be ready to give them by then.

The next day Julie and I drove about 140 kilometers north to Abomey.

The palace was once fabulous; each king added to it, and by the time of Glelé (1858–1889) it housed a court of ten thousand people, including eight hundred wives. His successor, Béhanzin, burned it in 1892 to keep it from falling into the hands of the French. What's left, courtyards and the additions built by Ghézo and Glelé, has been restored as a museum. From the outside, the palace is big but unimpressive, the usual rusty stucco wall surrounded by an empty expanse of red clay. Inside, however, in contrast to both the forlorn Ouidah and the exploited Ganvié, the palace is a well-kept and well-presented historical monument. Admission was 100 francs, the guide was a serious historian, and most of the other visitors were African. The collection includes the thrones of the kings, funerary paraphernalia, and the china, guns, and other European goods collected by the kings in trade and tribute. Most celebrated are the bas-reliefs and tapestries depicting the dynasty's history. I especially liked the big black umbrellas appliquéd with the kings' symbols. Unfortunately photography is not permitted inside the palace. I asked why and was told that some European had made his photographs into postcards without asking permission or sharing royalties.

If Americans know anything about the kings of Dahomey, it's their excesses—wives by the hundreds, human sacrifice, and an army of "Amazons." But the theme of the tour in postcolonial and Marxist Benin was their quest for autonomy. The Fon organized a state to protect themselves against the raiding Yoruba, and under Ghézo they succeeded in stopping the payment of tribute. They kept the European traders under strict control and exacted heavy taxes for the privilege of trade. In a vast Soviet-style square elsewhere in Abomey, there's a statue of Béhanzin, who held off the French bravely though temporarily. The guide used a Dahomean proverb to explain the dynasty's principle of government: The state is like a calabash of water full of holes; every citizen has to put his finger in a hole to keep the king's power, which is the life of the state, from being wasted. Thus personal infractions (like sleeping with the king's wives) were considered national treachery, and the sacrifice of individual citizens was considered to be for the good of the citizens collectively (though in practice most of those ritually sacrificed were outsiders captured for that purpose). Ghézo believed that some of the murderous customs were unnecessary and tried to reduce the extent of judicial and ritual killing, but he had to promote the slave trade to support the court, armies, and ceremonies he knew were necessary to maintain his power. He seems to have had a lot in common with many a modern African president who claims to respect human rights but believes that the security of the state rests in his person, exacts economic tribute in the form of a percentage of aid dollars and exports, and punishes perceived disloyalty with prison or death.

On a shady street outside the palace, we noted the symbols of Benin's current government—portraits of Marx, Lenin, Stalin, Mao, and the president, Kérékou—painted on the side of a school.

While we were buying bread and oranges for lunch, a masked dancer, draped in one of the traditional tapestries appliquéd with symbols of the kings, whirled through the market at the head of a procession. Julie warned me not to take photographs. She said if I did, they wouldn't come out. I grabbed one hastily from the back.

Then we hit the road home to get to the border before it closed at dark. On the way, boys leaned into the road waving dead agoutis by their tails. As we waited to cross the one-lane bridge over the Mono River at Grand-Popo, Julie bought a basket of crabs from other boys thrusting them through the car windows. Back in Lomé, we had dinner (not agouti) at Keur Rama, which is beginning to seem like mom's kitchen after a trip.

SUNDAY, JANUARY 8

"A & P"

✉ ✉ ✉

Back in class this week, Mr. Dogbé in the front row of American lit asked what I thought of the class. I said I thought they were terrific. Their English is good enough for me to speak normally; they're keeping up with five times the usual reading load; and, despite long practice in taking dictation, they're remarkably willing to venture into discussion.

That day we talked about Updike's story "A & P," in which the nineteen-year-old narrator, Sammy, quits his job as a checker at the A & P to protest the manager's embarrassing three girls who have come in in bathing suits by telling them, "Girls, this isn't the beach." I like the story partly as nostalgia. Achebe paints the bamboo beds, palm-oil lamps, and goatskin bags furnishing an Ibo *obi*; Updike, the green-and-cream checkered rubber-tile floor, the bow-tied checkers, and the framed statement of "Our Policy" of the classic American supermarket. Look, class, America has village institutions, too, and writers as interested as Achebe in preserving them for posterity.

The story is also good for generating a discussion of heroic values. Sammy sees his exit as a reenactment of the end of a western: "I just saunter into the electric eye in my white shirt that my mother ironed the night before." I asked the students whether they thought Updike approved or disapproved of Sammy's decision to quit. American students usually say he approves. Sammy sticks up for his principles; he is an individual, even if that costs him something. They don't question his principles or see any irony in the fact that this hero's sunset is an electric eye and his mother irons his shirts.

But the Togolese students thought Updike disapproved. Mr. Dogbé believed the manager's objection, "Sammy, you don't want to do this to your Mom and Dad," expressed Updike's view that, even though it's good to be original, it's more important to conform to social norms.

116

"Aha," I said, "note the cultural differences. American readers believe Updike values individuality; you believe he values social norms."

But Mr. Améyou, who has a difficult relationship with social norms, had a more interesting reason for thinking Updike disapproved. He pointed to the last sentence: "I felt how hard the world was going to be to me hereafter." He couldn't imagine how *choosing* to make life harder for oneself could be admired.

Ms. Agbodo observed, "It's easier for someone to challenge social convention in the U.S. than in Togo, where if you do so you will go to prison and your mother will never see you again."

Mr. Améyou added: "The difference is that in the U.S., society is society; here it's Somebody. There there are rules; here only Somebody. If I wanted to get into trouble all I'd have to do is go out into the street and say this *animation* [the parade for National Liberation Day next week] is not a good idea. I'm not kidding; if I did say that I'd be in big trouble. Even for saying it in this classroom. If Somebody says it's a good idea for students to march on Le Treize Janvier, it's a good idea."

In fact, I think, Mr. Améyou does come close to choosing the harder path.

Yesterday, Amy and I spent the whole day, seven-thirty A.M. to after seven P.M., on the panel interviewing students who want to go to the U.S. on the International Camp Counselor Program. Those selected will spend the summer meeting American kids' assumptions head on.

Afterward, Amy came home to supper with me and told me about a Chadian student in one of her classes. Amy had just learned that the student had *no* money and had had none since she arrived in early October. Her French scholarship hadn't come through, and she had no way of contacting anyone in Chad, where there's a civil war. She didn't have money to take a taxi to the American Cultural Center to get books she needed to write a paper and hadn't eaten in two days. Amy bought her a load of groceries in SGGG, on the theory that food is harder to refuse than money. In SGGG Amy ran into Rama, who when she heard the story bought her a bagful too. I sent money on the theory that money from a stranger is too hard to give back. The student also has not heard from her family since she left Chad.

This is individualism African style.

Le Treize Janvier

✉ ✉ ✉ ✉ ✉ ✉

Yesterday was National Liberation Day, the anniversary of the 1967 coup that brought Eyadéma to power. Soon after New Year's, the banners over the main streets proclaiming "Joyeux Noël" and "Bonne Année" were replaced by others of nationalistic self-congratulation. They are all in pairs: the banner over one lane commends Togo or the RPT; the one over the other lane attributes Togo's achievements to Eyadéma—for example, on the right, "TOGO, HARBOR OF PEACE," and on the left, "VIVE EYADEMA, MAN OF PEACE." My favorite says, "THANKS TO EYADEMA, GARANTOR OF OUR ECONOMIC INDEPENDENCE." Togo's national debt is 99 percent of its annual GNP.

As soon as school resumed after New Year's, classes were cancelled several afternoons a week so students could practice for the parade, the main event of the holiday. Since my classes are all in the morning, they weren't affected until the last week. Two of my American literature students met me outside the classroom on Wednesday to tell me that classes had been cancelled for an extra practice. I asked if they were going to march in the parade. Oh, no. Were any class members? I was thinking that since this was a small class, we might meet anyway if no one was involved in the parade (momentarily forgetting that if any assemblies are officially cancelled, holding them is considered subversive, which is why the students had waited *outside* the classroom). Well, the students answered, the women were obliged to participate because there were so few of them and the authorities wanted to show them off. Britt and Amy say that several mornings they've been awakened at five by soldiers stamping into their villa shouting, "Get up, get up, time to practice for the parade!"

My students and Togolese friends discouraged me from watching the parade in person. The route is so short, they said, you'd have to get there at dawn to get a place where you could see; you shouldn't park a car anywhere near the parade route and there will be no taxis to be found; you'd have to stand jammed in a crowd under the hot sun for six hours and it's not safe to take a camera. Watch it on television, they said, that's what we all do. So about mid-morning I dropped in on Vera and Philippe, who have a television. I knew they'd be watching the parade, knew I'd be welcome, knew I'd be invited to lunch, and realized how nice it was to know these things.

When I arrived, Vera and Mercy (who catered my housewarming party) were sprawled listlessly in front of the television. On the screen, contingents from every school in Lomé were marching past the reviewing stand swinging their arms up to shoulder level. The university students were all wearing blazers. No students wear blazers to class, no one need ever wear a blazer in this climate, but for some reason, university status required blazers. Other groups followed: Catholic diocesan officials, representatives of the Muslim community, representatives of the government labor union, regiment after regiment of the Union Nationale des Femmes Togolaises, and troops of young people whose T-shirts proclaimed them *militants animateurs*—cheerleaders for the government who perform at airport welcome ceremonies, international conferences, and the like. One troop wore pants made from a print commemorating the visit of François Mitterand to Togo, with photographs of the two heads of state positioned like knee patches, Eyadéma on one knee, Mitterand on the other. The dull succession of marching troops was broken only toward the end by groups of folk dancers from various regions and the "minigovernment" of children dressed to represent government officials—the Togolese equivalent of Tom Thumb and Lavinia Warren.

Throughout the morning, friends of Vera and Philippe dropped in and out. There were no introductions, and their desultory conversations were in Mina, so I had nothing to do but watch the parade. During a brief interlude without visitors, Vera asked me to stay to lunch. As soon as the parade ended at noon, the replay began. Philippe, who had returned from somewhere, moved a small portable TV and some living room chairs out to the terrace, where we watched the parade over again from its 8:00 A.M. beginning. Gradually the visitors cleared out and it appeared that only Vera's brother Stephen, visiting from Accra, would be staying to lunch, which was still not in evidence.

"What shall we do tonight?" asked Philippe, instantly extending the day.

I suggested we go to see *On Golden Pond* at the Vingt-Quatre Janvier and ask Kay, who I know gets depressed staying home alone on weekends, to join us.

Philippe suggested we go dancing.

After awhile, he asked if I would take him downtown.

I wasn't crazy about leaving the comfortable terrace and driving into the parade crowds on an unspecified errand, but even if I hadn't dropped in in expectation of lunch, I couldn't refuse. "Where do you want to go?" I asked.

"I'll show you," he said.

We stopped first at his mother's house. I was introduced, then they spoke in Mina. Then his uncle's house; the uncle wasn't home, Philippe left a message with his cousin. Then he said, "Let's go see Kay."

Kay seemed delighted to see us. She whipped up a blender full of orange juice. After awhile, Philippe asked if she would like to go to the movies with us. She declined. We visited a bit longer before Philippe got up to leave.

When we returned to the house, close to three, lunch was ready—*foo-foo* (yam pounded to a glutinous consistency, somewhat like bread dough) with peanut soup in honor of the holiday. I like *foo-foo*; the soup was good; Stephen was good company; and the conversation was in English. It would have been a very pleasant lunch except for Mercy's ambiguous position. She didn't seem to know whether she was a servant or family member. She had prepared and served the lunch and I could see her debating whether to bring out a chair for herself or not. She did, but then sat on the edge of it. Vera gave her no help.

Mercy is in Togo illegally trying to find work because things are so bad in Ghana. She's Vera's sister's friend, but since her sister doesn't have her own house, Vera has to take Mercy in. Outspoken Vera and obsequious Mercy are an ill-matched pair. Each provokes what she finds most irritating in the other. Vera admits that Mercy makes herself useful, but she resents having her around. She thinks Mercy ought to take a job as a cook for an expatriate family rather than depend on charity until she finds a job to her liking. Mercy resents Vera for trying to push her into a job as a domestic servant, which she thinks would prevent her from ever getting a profes-sional catering position and—I bet she sees this, too—keep her forever Vera's inferior. Mercy feels she has nowhere else to go; Vera is obliged to keep her sister's friend as long as she needs to stay.

After lunch, I went home for a couple of hours, during which time Philippe telephoned (having taken a taxi downtown to his office to make the call) to say that we would go to the movies instead of a nightclub because he'd been unable to find the friend I didn't know he'd been looking for as a partner for me.

Three of the four movie theaters in Lomé that middle-class Togolese and *yovos* attend are located within a couple of blocks at the end of the rue de Commerce. When we'd parked the car, Vera led us around from one to another studying the posters. She passed up *On Golden Pond* and a French romantic comedy and chose a spaghetti western. I told myself I should regard it as a French lesson and try to pay attention, but as absurdities unrolled on the screen, my mind wandered to Vera and Mercy and the students marching in blazers and I wondered how many other people today were feeling less liberated than manipulated.

Maîtrise

✉ ✉ ✉

Yesterday I suddenly felt at home. I was meeting Lee Ann for lunch at the Relais de la Poste. We'd been to enough restaurants to know our favorite. I knew how to get there without getting stuck at the roadblocks that guard the president's route back and forth to lunch. I knew which traffic lights didn't work and how to tell what color the light would be if it were working, how to talk to the car guard and how much to offer him, what to order in the restaurant. And Lee Ann and I knew each other well enough to talk about ourselves instead of the English Department and the Cultural Center. Nothing special happened, but everything seemed to come together.

Then in the evening Dagadou and Koami Johnson came over to talk about the possibility of offering a *maîtrise* in American literature, which is part of what's made me think about staying another year. Theoretically the department offers a *maîtrise*, which involves seventy-five hours of class and the writing of a thesis, in each of its specialties. They've offered one erratically in linguistics and in African literature, but never in American. It's a logical program for a Fulbrighter to develop, and I thought it would be fairly simple. The department could set some goals for the degree, and I could survey the resources available at the American Cultural Center, propose a couple of courses that would focus and fill in the students' spotty background, and prepare a brief guide to carrying out a research project. If I were to stay on next year, I could get it started; if not, my successor would have the necessary information.

Very good plan, said Dagadou, but the government insists that a *maîtrise* be offered during school vacations at Christmas and Easter so potential students teaching in the north can take part.

But, said I, you can't fit seventy-five hours of class into two weeks, especially holiday weeks. That would amount to a seventy-five hour, non-stop lecture. The teacher would do all the work because the students would have no time between classes. And no Fulbrighter would agree to that schedule because Christmas and Easter are the only times we have to travel.

True, true, said Koami.

And besides, I asked, aren't most of the potential *maîtrise* candidates right here in Lomé?

Yes, said Dagadou, they're this year's and last year's graduates who don't have jobs.

Well, I said, suppose a course were offered for three hours a week over the first semester, with a detailed reading list and study questions distributed at the beginning and a review session over Christmas for those who missed the classes?

Very logical, said Koami. In the past, we've even offered to hold these classes on Saturdays so teachers from the north could come down Friday afternoon, go to class on Saturday, and return Sunday. But the answer has always been no. The government is too sensitive about anything that suggests regional favoritism.

In short, if something isn't as convenient for northerners as for southerners, southerners can't have it either. If Koami and Dagadou can't persuade or get around "the government," I don't know what I can do. I don't even know who is speaking for "the government." The *directeur* of the EDL? The *recteur* of the university? Some Education Ministry official? I'll go ahead and work on a proposal, but I can see that my staying another year wouldn't put it into practice.

It all makes me wonder what I'm accomplishing. Learning to adjust is an accomplishment for me, and I think individual students are benefitting from an outsider's perspective, but could I do anything in a second year that the next newcomer couldn't do as well? A lot of what I like here is being a visitor. That's what makes such a simple thing as meeting a friend for lunch seem significant and such roadblocks as the conditions on the *maîtrise* bearable: I do what I can but this department's curriculum is not finally my responsibility. But you can only be a visitor so long, and I wonder if I'd be any less of a visitor next year. Does it make any difference whether you stay two years or one if you're not going to say, this is home, this is where I make my career, this English Department *is* my responsibility? And in a country like Togo does accepting responsibility give you any scope to carry it out?

The slides I took in Benin came back yesterday. Remember the one I took of the dancing mask that Julie said wouldn't come out? It didn't. All the other shots on the roll are normal; this one has a big flash of red and yellow light.

The Doorbell
✉ ✉ ✉ ✉ ✉

In Togo the doorbell replaces the telephone, and mine rings all day long. Vendors offer pineapples, hand-painted tablecloths, and teak tea wagons; cooks, maids, houseboys, and gardeners ask for work; unemployed university graduates want to give my children lessons; the representative of the domestic workers' union comes to collect my quarterly contribution (he doesn't ask whether I employ a domestic worker, but whether I'm sure I have only one); an old woman collects bottles, which will reappear in the market filled with palm oil and peanuts; the neighborhood bag lady brings my "mail," papers dropped from the garbage truck.

At first, I didn't realize that answering the doorbell was part of Mahouna's job, and besides I was curious. Now I'm only too glad to leave the door to him. The trouble is that he's only here in the mornings, and my callers seem to have learned to come in the afternoon.

The only ones I really mind are the beggars. Flint made it seem easy to deal with them. They're mostly alcoholics, he said; have them sweep the driveway or clean up the area around the garbage baskets and pay them in food, not money. But it hasn't worked like that.

One evening last fall a friendly, self-assured man came to the door. "Don't you know me?" he asked. He said he was a *gardien* at the house across the street and also worked on the neighborhood garbage truck. His employer across the street had gone to Nigeria without paying the help, and now they had run out of money for food. Would I lend him 3,000 francs just till the end of the month, when he would get his garbage man's pay from the Caisse?

"You can see, the whole house is dark," he said, by way of proof.

I couldn't give him food; the sort of food I could come up with on the spot—bread and cheese and a few cans—would be too little and more

125

expensive than lending the money. "Well, I'm sorry your employer is so irresponsible," I said, "but I can't pay other people's employees."

"But, *mama*, it's just a loan. We are neighbors. You see me every day on the garbage truck. I will pay you back in two weeks without fail. And I will take extra care with your garbage." A hint at the alternative?

"Why do you come to me? I just moved here, and I don't know you. You must have friends in the neighborhood."

"Because you are good, I can see. You'd be surprised, people know. Now, that mademoiselle"—he gestured toward Régine's apartment—"her I know from head to toe. I won't have anything to do with her." Poor Régine.

In the end I lent him the money. I never really had a choice. I was just stalling to preserve the fiction of my autonomy. The last person you want to alienate is your garbage man. And you'd better keep the neighborhood *gardiens* on your side. And, maybe, since we would see each other often, he would even pay the money back.

A few weeks later, a pathetic man came to the door and said, "Don't you remember me?" His pants were gathered at the waist by a too-long belt. His dirt-gray shirt hung in flaps from his protruding collar bones. His crusty toes curled under nervously as he talked. He was a friend of the man who lived here before, he said. That man helped him often. Now he was desperate and had nowhere else to go. That man would have helped him. His daughter was sick, the doctor said she needed medicine that cost 2,500 francs and he needed 375 more to take her back to his village in a *taxi brousse*, he'd walk back to Lomé himself, he would get work, he would pay back the money, but he needed it now or his daughter would die. He snuffled and sprayed through the gaps in his teeth and wrung his hands and seemed on the brink of tears.

When I could get a word in edgewise, I said, "But the hospital treats people for free, doesn't it?"

He had spent his last 200 francs on the entrance fee, but medicine was extra, and . . .

I didn't know the details of hospital policy, so couldn't challenge him on that. "But I don't know you at all. You must go to someone you know. I have enough to do to help the people I know," I said, thinking of my neighbor the garbage man.

His mother-in-law would help, but she was sick herself, and that man before was his only friend in Lomé, and . . .

I wonder if Flint was really as cool with his callers as he claimed. And

I wonder what makes me so angry about them. At home I write checks willingly for much larger amounts. In a way, the doorbell beggars are like the dinnertime phone callers at home who ask you to buy lightbulbs from the blind or tickets to the policemen's ball. These callers feign a personal relationship, too: "How are you this evening?" But the Lomé beggars insist on one. To them you can't say, "I'm sorry, but I never buy anything over the phone," or "I'm sorry, but my charity budget is already allocated." You can't stand in the doorway of a forty-thousand-franc-a-month apartment, next to a million-franc car, and say you can't help. It's no good giving reasons for refusing; for every reason they have a refutation. You can either comply—and get known as a sucker—or slam the door and feel like Scrooge.

My neighbor the garbage man waved and smiled when he saw me after I lent him money, and the litter around the garbage baskets disappeared. He did eventually repay the loan and has since borrowed the same amount again. The pathetic man came around later with a basket of eggs—not, he hastened to assure me, to try to sell me eggs, but to show me that his mother-in-law had given him eggs to sell so he could repay me.

This week the pathetic man came back, more abject than ever. He couldn't repay the loan, he snuffled, he'd tried to earn money, didn't I remember the eggs? But now he had TB and couldn't work (which could be true, he looked sick enough) and his wife in the village had no food (which could also be true, food supplies are running low for subsistence farmers), and he was desperate, he hadn't eaten himself since yesterday, he had nowhere else to turn, I was his only friend in Lomé, he'd do any job I wanted, but I had to give him 3,000 francs to buy food for his wife.

This time I was going to be smart and firm. "I can't give you any more money," I said, taking advantage of the unrepaid loan; "I haven't got endless money to give away. And there's no job you can do for me that's worth 3,000 francs. But if you sweep the driveway, I'll give you some food."

No, no, that wouldn't do. What he had to have was money to buy yams for his wife.

"Okay, okay, sweep the driveway and I'll give you a thousand francs. That will buy three yams. If you need more, you'll have to go somewhere else."

He pushed the broom around the driveway awhile looking as though he was about to expire, and I brought him a thousand francs. "But what about the food you promised?" he whined.

I went upstairs, made him a sandwich, handed it over, and closed the door. Somehow this man who had no claim on me beyond previous capitulation had made me feel manipulated and mean at the same time.

When another stranger showed up at the door yesterday and said, "Don't you remember me?" I was not encouraging.

"Don't you remember? I came here last September to ask for a job, and you said you didn't have a job for me, but you wished me luck. Now I've found a job and I've come to thank you for your good wishes." He gave me a card with a photograph of roses and a quotation from *Le Petit Prince*, which I recognized because just a couple of weeks ago I saw a stage adaptation of it at the French Cultural Center. The quotation was the "secret" the Fox tells the little prince to sum up a lesson on what connects people to each other: "On ne voit bien qu'avec le coeur. L'essentiel est invisible pour les yeux." We see well only with the heart. What counts is invisible to the eye.

Ecole Normale
✉ ✉ ✉ ✉ ✉

I'm just back from another trip to Benin, this time as a visiting lecturer. Togo and Benin are so closely related in so many ways—size, geography, history, indigenous and French-colonial culture—that the difference in audience reactions to a white American talking about black American life and literature is striking.

In Togo, my students are conscious of race, but to them "white" seems to have the neutral sense of "outsider" rather than the politically charged sense of "oppressor." For example, one day when I had dysentery and was too dizzy to continue class, Améyou, who insisted on going home with me to make sure I got there all right, said, oh yes, it was inevitable for *yovos* to get sick—as though *yovos* were an exotic species toward whom he felt friendly sympathy. The students don't associate race with point of view. Améyou and Ajavon come to me regularly after class to confirm their reading of the Afro-American literature they're reading with Miss Messan in opposition to hers. My British lit class found nothing to criticize in Shakespeare's characterization of Othello; and the fact that the characters were rich and white didn't keep them from relishing the village marriage game in *Pride and Prejudice*.

For the Atakpamé seminar, the *lycée* teachers asked me to talk about contemporary American race relations and responded appreciatively. They questioned whether American politics would ever be really open to blacks, but not my credibility or motives as an interpreter. If they made adjustments for the fact that the speaker was white, they did so privately.

In Marxist Benin, I stuck to literary topics I could back up very specifically. For the English Club at the Cultural Center in Cotonou, I gave an introduction to Afro-American literature that focused on several writers' use of conjure. I thought this angle would interest the audience because

129

conjure is based on voodoo, which originated and remains pervasive in this area, and it provided a way to consider Afro-American writers' relationship to traditional African culture. And I thought the audience would appreciate the conclusion that Chesnutt, Hurston, Walker, and Wideman have used conjure to represent the power of black people to prevail despite oppression.

The English Club turned out to be a group of about twenty gray-suited men—students and civil servants. They were interested, but not in Afro-American literature; they wanted to know about me. Why was I interested in black writers? What was I doing to combat racism in the United States? Was I interacting with Africans here?

At the Ecole Normale Supérieure in Porto Novo, I talked about the revolutionary critique of slavery in Afro-American folktales. This lecture was in French; it had been arranged only the day before; and the topic had been misannounced. I was insecure about my French, but not about the content of the talk, which showed the slave storytellers (and hence their analyst) to be as politically conscious as I figured the audience was. But the audience was having none of it. Why hadn't I talked on the announced topic? So what if folktales contained a political critique: Did it make the slaves revolt? My talk thus disposed of, did I believe African literature existed? I got this question wrong; the right answer was, no, African literature does not exist because so-called African literature is all in European languages.

I don't know how I'd have managed without the help of two university English professors who—anticipating problems?—sat on the platform with me, helped me pick out the questions from the surrounding *discours*, and followed up my answers with their own. At a dinner party in Cotonou that evening, they invited me to participate in the first conference of their newly formed Association for the Study of the Anglophone World, on the theme of Africa and the United States: Reciprocal Perceptions.

In fairness, the English Club may not have understood much of what I said. But I got the impression from both the friendly English Club and the hostile ENS students that what I said didn't matter; what they responded to was that I was white. And they understood "white" as "antagonist," even if the English Club did treat me as a curious exception.

Why the difference between Togolese and Beninois receptions? Has a dozen years of Marxist government made such a difference in Benin? Does it matter so much to individuals whether their dictatorship is leftist or rightist? Perhaps education is just where it does matter and that accounts for the sharp difference between the attitudes of the ENS students and the university faculty, educated before the coup.

On the other hand, maybe the difference has more to do with the fact that foreign and temporary as I am in Togo, I am still part of the community. I'm helping the students learn English and get a degree, which they consider steps to a better life, and, in contrast to Miss Messan, I'm interested in what they have to say. The teachers chose the topic of the Atakpamé lecture as one that would help them teach their prescribed curriculum. Mr. Adanlété, the philosophical vegetarian on the planning committee, even called on me a couple of weeks before the seminar to make sure I understood what the teachers wanted. I think in his gracious way he was trying to wrest for the teachers as much control as possible over the seminar imposed on them. So in Togo, because I live here, even a lecture has an element of dialogue and collaboration missing when a "visiting expert" comes in for a couple of days and talks on what she guesses might interest the audience. Perhaps the Benin audiences were reacting to the arbitrariness of edification imposed.

Véronique

⊠ ⊠ ⊠ ⊠

Monday I went back to my regular produce vendor after a season of apostasy.

You can buy produce from the women who carry it door to door in basins on their heads, but they don't have much variety and I'm seldom home when they come. The Grand Marché is too big and crowded, and there's no neighborhood market close to my house. So I've been going to a specialty produce market next to Marox, where most of the foreign service wives shop. This market has the biggest mangoes, the straightest carrots, the sweetest grapefruit, the whitest cauliflower, and the fiercest vendors in Lomé.

The first time I drove up, all the women who weren't actively engaged with another customer rushed the car. Before I could get out I was being pulled in several directions. "Madame, madame, buy from me. I have beautiful mangoes. Bon prix, bon prix." I thought I could placate everyone by buying something from each. This was a mistake, a gross violation of the rules. No one can understand how I got away with it that time. You are supposed to pick one vendor and buy from her exclusively. The second time I went, I was mobbed again, but this time one very large woman with what I now know is a permanent scowl had something specific against me. She said that last time I had bought from everyone else but her. In the moment of tension in which I was supposed to respond, Véronique came and rescued me. In that way, I became Véronique's *bon client*.

That first time, when she realized I didn't have one of the big inverted-lampshade baskets customers keep in their cars to carry their purchases home in, she gave me one. She dismissed my concern about returning it to her, but she knew full well that the need to return it would bring me back. Buying produce from Véronique is a little like going visiting. She comes flying out to the car calling, "Madame, madame, bonjour! Bonne arrivée!";

takes the basket from my hands; and leads me back to her stall inquiring about my health and telling me what special treats she has that day. I ask her about her family, and she asks me how things are going at the university. We compliment each other on new clothes. Véronique informs me about the seasons, hardly distinguishable to me. She told me in October that tomatoes would be scarce by December; she promises another mango season in June. At Véronique's you don't need to squeeze and sniff the fruit and guess how ripe it is; she tells you this one is *pour aujourd'hui*, that one *pour demain*, and a third *pour après demain*. When I want something Véronique doesn't have, she gets it from another stall; when Véronique is not there, her "sister" Elisabeth takes care of me.

The trouble with buying from Véronique is that she's in charge. I don't so much pick out what I want as strive to decline what I don't. Her approach to bargaining is not to lower the price but to throw in more goods. If I want a papaya and think 300 francs is too high, I end up with two papayas for 500 francs. When the same thing happens with lettuce, tomatoes, avocados, and oranges, and Véronique persuades me that her current shipment of grafted mangoes from Upper Volta may be the last of the season, and, what? have I never tried *corosoles?*, I really must, and because I'm such a *bon client*, she'll give me three cucumbers for just 100 francs instead of 200, I take home more food than I can possibly eat before it spoils. If I succeed in saying no to something Véronique proposes, that's what she throws in at the end "for dash." My dash is to give her six-year-old niece 10 francs to carry the basket to the car.

I tried being confidential with Véronique, told her that I lived alone and could use only small quantities. She nodded in sympathetic understanding and told me that she herself had left an abusive husband. But her understanding doesn't affect her sales technique.

It's a complex psychology Véronique uses. She appeals to a sense of thrift (or greed), but she also implies that I naturally want the best and would rather give excess to the servants she assumes I have than run short. She knows that a hundred francs more or less doesn't make any real difference to me and that, since we have a conversational relationship, and since I can afford it, my sense of politeness will allow me to fight only so hard. I arrive sweaty and harried, the working woman picking up groceries on her way home, and she treats me like a fine lady.

About Christmas, an outlet for a farmers' cooperative opened in the little shopping center in the *cité*, and I began shopping there, first occasionally and then regularly. I was tired of having fruit spoil in the fridge, tired of walking empty-handed behind a six-year-old while she staggered under my basket, tired of being a fine lady courted and manipulated. At the co-op, I can stick to my list, pick out the tomatoes I want, buy one papaya, know that the price per kilo is the same for me as for the Togolese hairdresser in the shop upstairs. But the carrots at the co-op tend to be gnarled; the onions may be soft; and the day I was having a dinner party they didn't have any avocados *pour aujourd'hui* or any mangoes at all. So I'm back to Véronique.

"Oh, madame, madame!" she cried as I drove up, "where have you been?"

"En voyage," I replied.

As I drove home with my overloaded basket, I suddenly understood one of the stories in the collection I'm teaching in British lit, Somerset Maugham's "The Force of Circumstance." In it, a young British colonial officer, who has lived for ten years as the only white person on a remote station in Malaya, brings back his new English bride. The two are completely happy until the bride learns that the silent Malay woman who appears around their house with silent "half-caste" children is her husband's former mistress. The husband tries to intimidate the Malay woman into leaving him alone and to make his wife understand the loneliness that led him to do what five out of six single colonial officers do, but the wife cannot bear to touch the man who has been intimate with a "black" woman and is also appalled at his callousness toward his "wife" of ten years and his own children. They live in polite estrangement for six months; then, one dawn, the bride returns to England. That night the oldest child appears in the doorway. The man sheds hot tears of defeat and concedes, "She can come back."

When I first read the story, I didn't see a point. The careless officer and his racist wife didn't interest me, and I didn't see how they would interest my Togolese students, who might rather identify with the Malay woman. Véronique made me think of the Malay woman. She never speaks, but the colonial officer himself unknowingly provides a clue to her point of view. When his wife asks if the woman is jealous, he says, "I daresay there were all sorts of perks when she was living here, and I don't suppose she much likes not getting them any longer." What's "perks" to him is a livelihood to her and her family. They understand that the colonial relation makes them poor and the Englishman lonely, so they take advantage of his loneliness to relieve their poverty. When an English bride arrives and upsets the balance, the Malay woman understands that the tangle of colonial idealism and racism will make the English woman sympathize with her and at the same time shrink from the man she's touched. It's not the force of circumstance that breaks up the English couple's marriage; it's the force of colonialism, which they themselves embody.

Véronique is ebullient where the Malay woman is silent; buying mangoes is not marriage; and Togo is technically no longer a colony. But like the characters in the story, Véronique and I are locked into positions of economic power and dependency established by colonialism. Like the Malay woman, Véronique uses her understanding of the gap between us to make as much money—and thus close the gap as far—as she can. I don't want to be a fine lady, but I'm white and drive a car. Véronique is only treating me the way generations of Europeans have made it advantageous for colonized people to treat them. She may not like her role either, but it brings her more money than she'd get if she let me shop as though I were in a supermarket. She may even think of the unknown cooks and housekeepers who get to take home an occasional ripe papaya thanks to her sales insistence. This is the hardest thing about living in a poor country—being taken for someone you don't recognize, or, worse yet, would repudiate.

Breakdowns
✉ ✉ ✉ ✉ ✉

Britt and Amy now have keys to my apartment so they can come here when they need a little space or privacy. They don't complain about each other to me, but they generally come here alone. Britt often drops by at midday on her way to or from the pool. Amy is sometimes here when I come home in the afternoon. Her books and notebooks will be spread out on the dining table, but she'll be reading one of my magazines. "Oh, Susan," she said once. "I just love your *New York Times Book Review*. It's in English and it has nothing to do with Togo!"

When I came home this afternoon, Amy greeted me at the door with wet hair, and the shower was running.

"We didn't think you'd mind, Susan. We haven't had water in our villa all week, and we finally couldn't stand another day without a shower."

When Britt got out of the shower, they told their story.

"Well," began Britt, "Monday morning when the fan wasn't turning, we thought, ho hum, another blackout, pas grande chose, c'est l'Afrique. I went off to the library to study—"

"But then," Amy continued, "some big sweaty men with wrenches came and started hacking away at the outside water pipes. Marceline came running into the room screaming, 'Nous sommes perdues, nous sommes perdues, apportes des sceaux!' [We're lost, we're lost, bring buckets!] The brutes took just enough pity on us to let us fill our buckets from the last drizzle—then *fini*. They handed us a bill and left."

"Would you believe?" demanded Britt, "The university hasn't been paying the water and electricity bills for months!"

"That night," Amy continued, "nobody could study because there were no lights—"

"It's *exam* week!"

"—and everybody was pissed about their meat spoiling in our fridge, so Irène decided to see what she could do. She went to the old juice-box and, knowing nothing about electricity—"

"But plenty about psychology!"

"—found a lever that said NE TOUCHEZ PAS and pulled it, and the fans and the lights came on. Everyone ran out onto the porch and hugged Irène and everybody else. Then we had to elect someone to tell the housing office what was happening. An election means that everyone nominated has to explain why she can't do it, and the one with the weakest excuse gets stuck. They wanted Britt and me to go, but we convinced them we weren't assez fortes en français. Finally Aminata volunteered; she's too nice to try to get out of anything. She took the water bill to the housing office—"

"Where it's now probably buried under some pile of papers."

"What have you been doing for water?" I asked.

"This is the best part," said Amy. "At noon that first day—before Irène rescued the electricity?—Bernadette marched into our room and asked, 'What are you eating for lunch?'

"'I don't know,' I said. I was really planning to skip lunch to avoid the hassle.

"'You got some eggs? Well, put them in that pan there. We're going to my compatriot's house to fix lunch—we can't cook here with no electricity.'

"She marched me over to her Ivoirian friend's house down the street. While we were cooking our eggs in his kitchen, she told me we were going to take our showers and get water there, too. She said, 'The Togolese girls have their families, but you have us.'"

"So every night," said Britt, "we walk over to this guy's house, fill buckets with water, hoist them up on our heads, and walk home. The kids in the street go crazy. The *yovos* are carrying water on their heads just like good Togolese women!"

"We haven't actually taken showers at the Ivoirian's house," Amy added. "We've been taking bucket showers at home. Which I kind of enjoy. It makes me feel more like I really belong here, and it's amazing how much you can do with one bucket of water."

"Well, I wouldn't *choose* a bucket shower over the real thing," said Britt.

"No," agreed Amy. "But I wouldn't have missed Marceline running around screaming 'Nous sommes perdues!'"

Naturally, they stayed to dinner. We had a lot to talk about, as I hadn't seen them since before I went to Benin, and they'd both been depressed for the last month. They tend not to tell me their problems till they can joke about them. This week's *coupages* seem to have cut more than the water and electricity.

"You have to come see our room," said Amy. "We've fixed it up." Tripping over each other and their stuff in that little hot box had to be depressing.

"Since I wasn't using my bed anyway, we moved it out," said Britt. "And we ordered two desks from the neighborhood carpenter—only 3,000 CFA apiece! They came yesterday. We put the hot plate and tea and stuff on one of them and the fridge in the closet. It's only a *little* awkward to have to open two doors to get into it."

"Actually," said Amy, "the closet door is usually open. That's what we hang our clothes on."

"Those that we hang up," corrected Britt. "Most of them are stuffed in our suitcases under Amy's bed. We've abandoned bandbox standards. Of course, *this* week, they're all in the laundry pile. Oh, and I forgot, we bought two lamps. So we actually have two desks—if we move the hot plate to the floor—and two lamps for studying *and* room to turn around."

"It's almost pleasant," said Amy. "I can't believe we waited four months to do this."

"Assiobo's exam has been postponed again," Amy offered later. "The one I was supposed to take at the beginning of February? That was postponed to this week because Assiobo went to Dakar? Now it's not till the end of March. I don't think I can study for that exam *again*. If he ever does give it, I think I'll just take it cold. So, I get low marks. Tant pis. Who in California will know the difference?"

"And you *know* they're not going to flunk the *yovos*," Britt reminded her.

"I think the only schoolwork that's worth bothering about is our research projects."

Britt is studying the Green Revolution in Togo and Amy women in development. They've both met people at places like AID and the UN Food and Agriculture Organization who are helping them get interviews with people working in these areas and invitations to development projects. Much more interesting stuff than recramming dictated lectures for eternally postponed exams.

"Otherwise," said Amy, "I'm ready to learn how to make *foo-foo*!"

Economics
✉ ✉ ✉ ✉

Mahouna and I continue to surprise each other.

I started noticing lately that the half baguette I left from breakfast was often only a quarter baguette when I came home expecting to make a sandwich for lunch. I who freeze up when dinner party conversation turns to anecdotes about finding the gin bottle full of water or the cook's family's laundry in the washing machine began fretting about the disappearance of two and a half cents worth of bread. I didn't want to think I begrudged Mahouna a little bread, but it was irritating to come home and find what I'd planned on for lunch gone.

I didn't know what to do. If I spoke about it to Mahouna, he would think I was accusing him of stealing, and I would feel like a particularly petty example of the expat fixated on domestic theft. If I just started buying two baguettes every morning, without saying anything, I'd be left with a lot of day-old bread to send home with Mahouna. I'd be contributing to the image of the extravagant *yovo* and participating in the paternalistic colonial charade in which the master pretends not to notice that the servant is manipulating him—even though Mahouna had no intention to manipulate. I didn't think a quarter baguette was a very nutritious breakfast for Mahouna, if that's what it was serving as, and I didn't think he was comfortable with what he was doing, because he never took all of anything. I know he has some sense of nutrition because whenever I've invited him to share a breakfast or lunch with me and asked him what he'd like to drink, he's asked for milk.

I hadn't really decided what to do when, the other morning, the question just popped out: "Mahouna, do you eat breakfast before you come here?"

No, he said promptly, he had to leave home so early to get here by

7:30 that he wasn't hungry. Later in the morning he was hungry and he ate something here.

He was so honest it was easy for me to explain why I didn't think this procedure was very satisfactory.

Then he proposed a solution I wouldn't have thought of: Could he take a break in the middle of the morning to get a meal at the cook stand near the pool?

Of course. He's the one who decided to come half an hour early when I bought the car, and I often have to shoo him out half an hour after he's supposed to leave in the afternoon. Of course he could take a break when he got hungry. This way, he gets a real meal, I know what's in the refrigerator for lunch, and he and I are back to being employee and employer instead of dependent and *patronne*. I thought we were both relieved.

Later that morning I found him looking downcast and asked what was wrong. "J'ai honte," he said. I couldn't tell him *I* was ashamed to bring the whole matter up. I tried to explain that it wasn't a matter for shame, that we'd come upon a problem and solved it, but I'm not sure I succeeded.

A few days later, Mahouna asked for another advance on his pay. Back in September, shortly after we'd settled his salary, he asked me to advance him 60,000 CFA to help him set up a *boutique* for his beverage business. He said he'd pay the money back by taking only 10,000 instead of 20,000 francs a month in pay; he could get by on that because he had the beverage business and his afternoon job at the British School teacher's. He hoped to open the *boutique* by Christmas, and I'd be the guest of honor at the grand opening. I was a little nonplussed to face yet another unknown in the employer-employee relationship so soon after settling the hours-and-wages question. But Mahouna's ambition to become a *commerçant* instead of a *domestique* seemed worthy of support, and his pay-back plan sounded reliable, so I advanced him the money. The *boutique* hasn't opened—a carpenter has put him off for a more lucrative job, a permit has been delayed, etc.—but by the end of this month, the loan will be repaid.

Mahouna referred to this when he asked for another loan. He said, "After this loan is paid off, you will be here another three months, enough time for me to pay off a loan of 30,000. Since my extra money has been tied up in the *boutique*, I haven't had any to lend. Usually I lend money to people who can't pay their bills when they're due. I give them 1,000 francs and they pay me back 1,300 at the end of a month. If you lend me 30,000, I'll be able to make money lending money."

This time, for once, the answer was clear. "Mais non! Don't you realize you are asking me to lend you money *without* interest so you can lend it *with* interest? And the interest you're charging those poor people is incredible—360 percent!"

He said, yes, he saw, and went back to his work.

Later he came back to the bedroom where I was working at my desk and asked if I'd ever studied economics. I said, "No, why?"

He said, "Because you were able to explain to me about interest."

His moments of naïveté are startling because he's so accomplished and worldly in so many ways. In language, for example. I laughed when he told me with pride last fall that his French was *correct* because that doesn't sound like much of a claim in English. But "correct" is exactly right, and in French as a second language correctness is no mean accomplishment. He's correct in other ways, too. Perhaps this is why he was so downcast over the bread. He doesn't want to do anything incorrect.

I don't think about how correct Mahouna is until, occasionally, he lets loose—such as when he showed up in short shorts and a porkpie hat to take me to his house for dinner. Or when Britt and Amy told me that when they stay in my apartment when I'm away, he acts like their amorous classmates. He's making clear distinctions: He and I are both single and close in age, but I'm his employer; Britt and Amy aren't.

We talked once about being single. He asked me if it were *mal vu* to be single in the United States and if it were worse for a woman or a man. This is not the way other Togolese have inquired about my marital status. The usual question is, Why aren't you married? Mahouna was not only less personal but more willing to respect another person's choice and to accept other ways of doing things. He's well aware himself of the complexities of following a norm others take for granted. He said he'd like to get married in a couple of years, once the *boutique* is established, but he doesn't know how he's going to meet a suitable wife. He came to Lomé to make money, but without family here he has no one to matchmake for him. The hard work that would make him a good catch gives him no occasion to meet women in the *fonctionnaire* class to which he aspires and no time to develop close ties with the neighbors who might function for him as family. Besides, they may resent the fact that he makes money off their insolvency. And if they were to start matchmaking he might suspect their motives.

Hot Season

✉ ✉ ✉ ✉

I keep thinking it can't get any hotter, but it does. I spend every minute I'm home in my dark bedroom with the air conditioner and lights on. When the power went off for half an hour the other day, I realized how much my equilibrium depends on electricity. Everybody is waiting for the relief of the rains. The standard small-talk opener has become something like "I hear it rained last week in Abidjan."

In Lomé, it turns out, the hot season is also the robbery season, because in the country it's the lean season, which has turned Nick and Geeta and me into the Keystone Kops.

At first we paid no attention to the robbery gossip because, with all the villas around, who would bother the apartments? We're living so minimally, what do we have to steal? We thought the bars the Caisse installed last November were pointless. Then Merle's apartment in another block was cleaned out, and we discovered the purpose of the bars: They serve as a ladder to the second-floor balcony and easy access through the living room windows.

The obvious response was to hire a *gardien*, but none of us wanted to think of ourselves as the kind of people who have *gardiens*. Geeta suggested a homemade burglar alarm used in India—a string of tin cans across the entrance where an intruder would knock it down and create a clatter. So I strung some cans on a thread, and every night for a week or so I hung it across the living room windows. I had to close the louvers to lock the windows, turn off the air conditioner so I could hear if the cans were disturbed, and, because without the air conditioner mosquitoes would light, sleep under a sheet. Hot, hot, hot.

Then one evening Vitaly went upstairs from his bedroom and surprised a man on his way out the balcony door. The man dropped his loot and fled. What he had taken was food, and Vitaly said he was naked. Later when I asked Alidou about this, he said, yes, naked so no one could grab him by his clothes, and probably greased as well.

He was desperate, so now we were, too. We decided we had to break down and get a *gardien*. Vitaly and Régine agreed. But how to find one we could trust to keep thieves out rather than usher them in? How to check up on him while we were asleep?

The commandant of the gendarmerie lives across the street; we thought someone we found through him might feel supervised by him. The commandant produced a relative of his driver, whom we hired for a two-week trial period. From the beginning we knew we'd made a mistake. Whenever I got up in the night, I'd hear him snoring in my carport. When I opened the door to challenge him, he would wake up and deny he'd been asleep. When the two weeks were nearly up, I got up one morning and missed his snoring. I went outside and looked all around the building; he wasn't there. At six, when he was supposed to quit, he came strolling around the circle. By then, Nick and Geeta and Vitaly were all up and out, too. There had been a robbery on the other side of the circle, he explained, and all the *gardiens* had gone to try to catch the thief. Fine, we said, take us to the house, and let us talk to the owners. We're halfway around the circle, asking which house is it, when he says, well, the owners had been asleep, and the *gardien* didn't speak French, and . . .

Then the problem was how to get rid of him. Were we calling him a liar? We were just like all the others, didn't trust a man to know his job, here he was just trying to earn an honest living, how would we like to work all day and stay up all night? We were destroying his reputation, taking food out of his children's mouths, he'd never be able to get another job, and we would be to blame. Finally, we said, look, you're a fine *gardien*, we have no complaints, we just don't need you anymore; take the two weeks' pay and go. Now we really needed a *gardien*.

When I mentioned the problem to Kay, she said, for heaven's sakes, go to the embassy, they run a *gardien* placement service that screens applicants and checks up during the night on the ones they place.

The evening of the very day I asked for one, they sent us Dongo. He arrives at dusk and leaves at dawn. Every evening, I put a chair out for him; every morning, Mahouna brings it in. At intervals he walks around the building shining his flashlight into the bushes. The first night, he panto-mimed for me how he would lay into an intruder with his club. We've had no more incidents, and Dongo sitting in the driveway, bundled up in his jacket, wool cap pulled down over his ears, flashlight and club at the ready, is now part of what seems normal.

If we'd only realized from the beginning that anyone with enough to eat is the kind of person who hires a *gardien*.

Culture Crossing
✉ ✉ ✉ ✉ ✉ ✉

Last night Nick and Geeta and I went to the graduation recital of a drumming and dancing school for Europeans run by Nick's Ghanaian master-drummer friend Mustapha and his German wife, Heide. At first it was just funny and embarrassing: seminaked whitefolks prancing around to the laughs and whistles of a Togolese audience. But the whistles signified admiration, and after awhile it was clear that two of the students were really good, even by African standards, and the rest had obviously learned a lot.

Still it was bizarre. The dances have meaning in the context of African culture, but the performers had not been immersed in African culture; they'd been camping out on the beach for three months, and the culture they projected was closer to Club Med. For them, the dances represented a vacation from their own culture. At the same time, Togolese of their age and class would not be caught dead doing these dances. In the closest I've heard to a political discussion, a couple of René's businessmen friends, sitting around with a beer after tennis, were complaining that all the government's promotion of traditional culture is intended to distract people from the substantive issues. "Moi, je ne chante pas," spat out one of them. "Moi, je ne danserai jamais," concurred his friend. Maybe the audience was appreciating the parodic elements of the performance as well as the skill, as well as the performers' effort, however comical or qualified, to enter their world.

A spectacle like this makes you wonder who you are. We were European like the dancers but sitting in the audience, in judgment, like the Togolese. But none of us could have danced as well as the worst of these performers, so our judgment had more to do with how well they were representing us than how successfully they were imitating Togolese dancers. Nick was there as both kin to the performers—since he too is studying

African music—and a colleague of their teacher. After the dancing, he played guitar with Mustapha's group in a demonstration of the fusion of African music and Western instruments.

Who we are seems to depend so much on where we are. On stage, in the audience; in Togo, in the United States; downtown, at home. Nick and Geeta and I feel distant from the Lloyds' distance from Togo—until Togo tries to break into our house.

Nick has changed since he's been here. He's shaved off his beard (too hot, too hard to keep clean), cut his hair, and admitted a connection between drinking palm wine with the drummers and getting diarrhea. At first he was a magnet for con artists. Only recently he told me about one episode that dragged on for a couple of months.

"I'm standing by the road waiting for a taxi and this other guy waiting starts asking all about me. When I say I'm a musician, the guy says, 'You must come to my village, we have the best music and dancing, the village is remote, we have to go over rivers by canoe.' I think, 'Great! This is *just* what I came to Africa for' and invite the guy home to arrange it. He's real vague about where the village is but real specific about what I'm supposed to bring: my camera and tape player.

"Geeta is mad. She thinks I'm nuts to want to go to a backwoods African village because to her it's just like a backwoods Indian village, basically poor. And she doesn't believe the guy.

"So I talk to Alf, and he says it sounds suspicious; introductions are important. Ayité and this friend-of-a-friend at the Ministry of Culture say, if it were legit, the guy would ask me to bring an African friend, too.

"So now the guy is coming to pick me up and I don't want to go. Geeta says, '*You* deal with it.' When he comes, I say, 'I can't go, I have to go down to the Cultural Center because I'm expecting a call from home, somebody's sick.'

"He starts getting desperate: 'Look, I bought all this food.' He holds up a bag of rice. 'The whole village is making special preparations in your honor.'

"Finally I get him out of the house. Of course, it's Saturday, so when we get downtown and the center's closed, he says, 'We need to talk about our friendship.' And he tries to sell me this special magic that when I go back to the U.S. and a guy mugs me in the street it will turn his gun or knife to water.

"I say I don't need it, and the guy says, 'I need $500 to get a consignment out of customs. There's $1,000 hidden in it, I'll give you $600 back. I just need it for an hour. You Americans are all rich.'

"I say, 'No, I am but a humble student,' and the guy looks at me like I'm saying I don't breathe oxygen.

"My problem," he concluded, "was that I didn't know how to discriminate. I thought because I meant well toward others they would mean well toward me. I didn't realize what it meant to be the only person in people's lives who represented a higher standard."

Geeta is the one having the trickiest time with relative identity. As an upper-middle-class Indian, she was used to feeling like one of the colonized in relation to "whites" in India but like an aristocrat in relation to the millions of servants and squatters. To the Togolese, though, she's white. At first, Nick's drumming friends were standoffish to her. They distrust Indians because the Indians own so many of the shops. But they also think Indians, like Africans, do magic, only better. She's the one who finally got rid of the guy pestering Nick by intimidating him with threats of Indian juju. So suddenly she's got two new identities, white and a magician. She's also seeing a society much like the one she takes for granted in India from an outside point of view and finding that she doesn't like the clannish Indians here, who have tried to adopt her.

But she also teaches art and English part time at the British School and thinks that as far as Callie, Trevor, and Merle are concerned, she's black. They patronize her, which she finds funny, because she considers them lower middle class, but also infuriating. In a way her job there is a colonial situation. The Lloyds criticize her accent and her teaching, change the terms of the contract, and postpone paying her, but they keep her on because it's not easy to get someone who will put up with low pay and bad treatment. She stays because she'll only be here a little longer and the unfair pay she gets from them is better than nothing. It must be galling to the Lloyds to have someone whose accent they despise teaching English, and it's galling to Geeta to be told by Philistines how to teach art.

What saves all of us is long visits in their apartment or mine that start out with an afternoon errand, stretch through Nick's return from his drumming lesson, a pot-luck supper, and many Bières Bénin, and dissect our relationships with Togolese friends and acquaintances, other expats, parents, siblings, and former lovers. For a while I thought of these evenings as an escape from what I was really here for, which was to get to know Togolese culture. Now I think they're part of the purpose. Because the interesting thing about living in Lomé is not simply Togolese culture, which we can never be part of anyway, but the intersections of different cultures, which include Bombay bourgeois, Cambridge counter, and American academic as well as Togolese of various classes, British colonial, and all the rest.

I've just finished a book called *An African in Greenland* by Tété-Michel Kpomassie, a Togolese who at the age of sixteen read a book about Eskimos and decided he had to go to Greenland. He made his way over eight years via Ghana, Senegal, France, Germany, and Denmark to Greenland, where he traveled for over a year from the depressed towns of the south to the frozen north, living with Eskimo families. I was interested, first, in the depiction of life for a teenager in Lomé about the same time I was a teenager in Connecticut. (When he fell out of a coconut palm he was taken to the python priestess, not the hospital, but he also went into town and browsed in bookstores.) Second, in the way Kpomassie makes a European reader who probably considers him primitive when he's in Togo identify with him when narrator and reader together confront meals of raw whale skin and seal blubber and hospitably shared towels and girlfriends. But I was most interested in the way the narrator's own identification slips around. Brought up in a traditional African family, he went to a French school, spent several years in Europe, landed in Danish-colonized southern Greenland, and made his way to the more authentically Eskimo north, and he identifies at different times with all these homes. At times he proudly explains Togolese culture, at other times repudiates it (he left home because his father was about to dedicate him to the python cult). Shortly after he arrives in Greenland, he goes to a French movie he's already seen because "this old film represented my only remaining link with the European world." Later, he explains his determination to go to the northernmost settlement as "a desire to find some last fixed point which would be neither southern Greenland nor Africa, and above all not Europe!" But before long, he returns to Europe, where, we learn from the introduction, he settled. I suspect if I'd read this book last year in the United States I would have found the point of view confused. Now it seems perfectly normal.

The Route d'Atakpamé

✉ ✉ ✉ ✉ ✉ ✉ ✉ ✉

Whenever I turn onto the Route d'Atakpamé from the quiet *cité* I feel as though I'm jumping into a Woody Allen film—anything can happen, and whatever it is, I'm watching it and part of it at the same time. A man pedals around the Rond Point, back straight, eyes front, balancing a kitchen table on his head. At the light at the Boulevard Circulaire, I pull up behind a chic woman on a motorcycle—long tight skirt hiked up over her knees, high heels hooked over the pedals, head encased in helmet. Without taking her eyes off the light, she reaches into her shoulder bag and tosses a coin to the beggar sitting on the corner.

In September I watched the median strip of the four-lane stretch between the Rond Point and the president's house grow gradually pink and yellow as workers planted two miles of flower cuttings one by one and watered them by hand. One day, as my attention wandered on the drive downtown, a car passing me suddenly cut in front, and oncoming traffic filled the passing lane. They were painting lines on the northbound side of the median; a branch laid on the pavement had diverted traffic to the southbound side; southbound got no warning.

About the same time, I could look off to the right and watch a low field gradually fill with water from the rains. As the field got wet, people started working it, planting something, tending it. If I drove downtown early in the morning, I'd see people squatting in the field; later in the day, they'd be standing ankle- and then calf-deep in the water, hoeing or transplanting. Were they growing rice, I wondered? And were they paying for a crop with schistosomiasis by standing in water used as a latrine? I never saw a crop or a harvest. As the rains ran down, the field dried up and the people disappeared.

After dark at exam times, students sit under the street lights, memorizing their notebooks.

Yesterday I was returning at dusk from Agouenyivé. It had been a long day. On my way to visit Madame Abidji, I'd found her walking out toward the Route d'Atakpamé to get a taxi into town, so I'd taken her into town, parceled out the visit between her errands, and driven her back up to Agouenyivé. I'd negotiated the railroad tracks four times without scraping the bottom of the car and was almost home when a policeman standing beside the road waved me down. He got into the passenger seat and told me to turn around and "follow that car." Had I seen what that driver had just done? He had almost caused an accident! We couldn't allow drivers like that to go unapprehended.

I wasn't sure which car he meant, or what infraction had been committed, but I made a U-turn and started north again. "Foncez, madame, foncez!" he urged.

The only other time I'd heard the verb *foncer* it was in the past participle in the notions department of a Paris department store. I was trying to match a button, and the clerk said that one possibility was "trop foncé," meaning in context "too dark." I supposed that the connection had something to do with profundity and that *foncez* meant "floor it." I tried to comply, but all my instincts were against speeding in front of a policeman and my sympathies with the driver under pursuit.

Eventually the car he was after stopped, without my having to attempt a high-speed chase. The policeman got out and said, "Merci, madame, you may go now." So I never found out what happened between the erring driver and the policeman, who, after citing him for an infraction, must have had to ask him for a ride back to town.

To the North
⊠ ⊠ ⊠ ⊠ ⊠

Finally, Nick, Geeta, and I are off on the trip we've been talking about for months, the Route Nationale No. 1, past Atakpamé, all the way north. I mean "finally" literally, as Nick and Geeta are leaving for Bombay this Sunday. I will miss them. We're having a wonderful time. We left Friday morning, got to Dapaong Saturday night, and are now having a rest day in Lama Kara on the way back. As usual in Togo, nothing has worked out quite as planned, but everything has worked out.

Friday noon in Atakpamé, we had a flat. I didn't realize it at first because we were on a cobblestone road, and drivers are always honking anyway. But the honkers kept after me till I figured it out—right in front of a gas station. The attendants changed the tire, then pointed out a tire repair shop, identified by a pile of truck tires, just across the road. While the tire repair artist clamped the patch to the tire over a little pot of fire, we joined his wife, baby, and friends hanging out in the shop listening to Afrique No. 1, the Africa-wide pop station from Gabon. We sat on a springy bench held up at one end by a wooden leg, the other by a pile of tires; another pile of tires served as an armchair. The radio was attached to the corrugated iron roof, which served as an antenna. The whole shop was a couple of feet below road level, so we had a mole's-eye view of the scooter, bicycle, and pedestrian traffic. Instead of going around Atakpamé, we watched Atakpamé going by. The repair that was supposed to take fifteen minutes took an hour and a half. The price was 800 francs plus "something to eat," which turned out to be 25 francs (which bought a bunch of bananas). The price of the tire change across the road had been "whatever you want." That the car was being taken care of was only an illusion, or an incidental; what was happening was that people were taking care of each other.

We'd planned to spend Friday night in the Bonne Auberge in Sokodé, but when we got there somebody who was supposed to have left hadn't because his car had broken down, so there were no rooms. The Swiss owner was regretfully conceding that we'd have to go to the government-run Hôtel Central when the thought occurred to him, why spend 8,000 CFA on an air-conditioned room when the electricity would be off (as it is everywhere except Lomé) between midnight and 8 A.M.? We should go to the Cercle de l'Amitié; he would send his *gardien* to show us the way.

At the Cercle de l'Amitié, a shuttered colonial house down an eroded side street past a mosque, everything was dark except for a little pool of kerosene lamplight on the terrace where a barefoot French couple, who turned out to be the managers, were sipping beer. To avoid paying for air-conditioning when the power was off after midnight, we'd come to the *quartier* whose turn it was to be *coupé* in the early evening as well. The Cercle was a simple place. Eight small rooms, furnished with a bed and table, period, opened off a wide tiled corridor. No wastebasket, no mirror. No screen, no fan, not even a top sheet against mosquitoes. The French couple seemed surprised when we asked for top sheets, toilet paper, candles, and matches for the mosquito coils we'd brought. We didn't bother to ask for towels and soap, which we'd also brought. They assured us it was cool at night and that with a coil, mosquitoes wouldn't bother us. But it was hot, and the coil didn't bother the mosquitoes. In the morning we discovered a wasp nest in the shower. The Cercle could have been charming if someone had bothered with details. As it was, the price, 2,000 CFA, suited the amenities.

The next morning we picked up a Peace Corps volunteer who'd been waiting outside the Bonne Auberge for two days for a ride to Lama Kara. We stopped in Bafilo, where we'd been told to seek out the dyers and weavers of Bafilo cloth, a heavy blue-, black-, and maroon-striped cotton woven in narrow strips, which was supposedly cheaper from the weavers than from the market. We didn't find any cloth for sale outside the market, but, with the help of Josh, our passenger, who spoke Kabyé, we had a wonderful tour of the back streets of Bafilo. The frail-looking old man we asked for directions hiked us through the clay streets to a weaving shop set up in the street itself, the warp yarns stretched for blocks down the middle. The weavers there (free to talk because boy apprentices were working the looms) directed us to a woman who worked inside and made a different, wider kind of cloth. She demonstrated her weaving and thanked us for our visit. On the back streets of Bafilo, where street and houses are the same clay color and one day is the same as the next, people are the source of interest and four *yovos* constitute an event. Adults greeted us; children trailed, showing off outsized flip-flops, school exercise books, baby brothers. They didn't ask for *cadeaux* and were thrilled to be given candy. At the market, a vendor of handsome but bulky and expensive Bafilo-cloth shirts seemed happy to have his shirts admired and his photograph taken without making a sale.

Saturday morning's drive took us into new terrain, mountainous and green from the new rains. South of Bafilo, one lane of the road passes through a dramatic fault. Truck carcasses dotted the slopes. We dropped Josh in Lama Kara before noon and thought of staying there to visit the nearby sites he recommended, but for some reason we felt like pushing on to the end of our route. Around Niamtougou, the land flattened out and the newly green savannah looked like a golf course studded with palms and clusters of round, thatched houses—Africa in Disneyland. After Kanté, the land became drier and rockier.

In the afternoon, we crossed the Keran National Park, a flat, scrubby game reserve, where we saw monkeys, baboons, wild boars, antelopes, and lots of deer. The sense of wildness there was compounded by the threat of vague government regulations. The speed limit is 50 kilometers per hour, enforced by time checks at entrance, midpoint, and exit. It's hard to keep to 30 miles an hour on an open road, and not knowing where the midpoint was, we were afraid we'd arrive too early. The police also checked bumpers and tires for signs of blood and hair. A permit is required for a "photo safari," and we didn't know whether that meant us or not, so we took photographs but kept our eyes out for other cars. Outside the park, we saw an elephant, just where the map shows a picture of one and within sight of a road sign that said "Danger Elephant." In Boumbouaka, a tree-shaded town south of Dapaong, women and children were washing clothes in what looked like an animals' shallow water hole. Children carried the wet clothes up the hill to the town in basins on their heads.

Travel in Togo isn't hard, but even with a map and a paved road it's improvisational, and when we got to Le Campement in Dapaong we felt as though we'd made it through uncharted territory. Le Campement had the character of a relay station on an overland expedition route. It had private baths and air-conditioning (till midnight), but none of the restrictions of hotel culture. The two owners served up rooms, drinks, food, plumbing repairs, and bush-driving advice. You could leave your food in their fridge and get beer all night long and breakfast from 3 A.M. Our companions for an evening in the bar were local prostitutes and weathered travelers. The focus of attention was a three-inch black scorpion in a cage on the bar.

On the way back south, we've been more relaxed. We pulled off the road for a picnic in the Keran reserve, which is probably more illegal than taking pictures, but no one bothered us. At Kanté, we turned off on a track into the Tamberma region and stopped at Titira, the first Tamberma village. The Tamberma live in fantastic turreted houses like miniature medieval castles, hunt with bows and arrows, and have only recently encountered Europeans. We didn't know how we'd communicate with them or even whether we'd find them. Steve Rosen, the AID officer, had said vaguely, "Be careful." We picked up a hitchhiker on the way, an old man with a machete who kept his feet tucked under him until Nick nudged them to the floor. We hoped he'd give us an introduction to the village, but he got out before we got there.

When we did reach the village, it was clear they'd seen tourists before. A man who spoke French took charge of us—showed the wood and mud construction of the houses, demonstrated how an intruder would have to stoop to enter and thus be vulnerable, offered a sample from the bin of baobab seeds. The guidebook had described a social structure as well designed as the houses; it mentioned family altars, a village square, a chief who is pleased to welcome visitors. We didn't see any of that, only sick and scrawny or healthy and grabby people. We'd given out balloons and candy when we arrived to show our goodwill. This turned out to be a mistake as more people kept showing up demanding *cadeaux*. Our guide kept them at bay until we were about to leave and it was clear the *cadeaux* were gone. We gave the guide 500 francs to distribute as he saw fit and hustled into the car. Back in Kanté, we stopped at a *buvette* to have a Coke and recover. It was distressing to realize that there was no way to encounter people across such a chasm of difference except as competing predators.

After an afternoon with the Tamberma, we checked into the international-class Hôtel Kara here in Lama Kara and succumbed to the comfort. This morning, we drove through Pya—the president's home village, with appropriate monuments—up a mountain track to Tcharé, a village known for its Monday market specializing in pots (made by the women on Tuesday, Wednesday, and Thursday) and hoe blades (forged by the men on Friday, Saturday, and Sunday). On a stop to admire the view of village rooftops nestled among the trees, we met a young woman walking to the market and offered her a ride. She spoke French because she'd almost finished the *lycée* before her father decided it was time for her to stay home and work. She said she had walked from Bassar the day before and was going to Tcharé to buy a water jar, an egg-shaped earthen pot about three feet tall and two feet in diameter. I'm not sure we got her story quite straight, because Bassar is almost a hundred kilometers away, even as the crow flies, but there's no doubt that she was going to walk back to wherever with the pot on her head. We picked up another woman carrying a pot up to the market. The pot was going to cost 500 francs; taxi fare from Bassar would have been 600. The market was hacked out of the side of the mountain; the pots threatened to roll down the slopes; the hoe blades were laid out on rock walls. Our passenger kindly stuck with us to interpret with the vendors, but when we were ready to leave declined a ride down the mountain because, though there were hundreds of pots available that all looked alike to us, the vendor she wanted to buy from had not yet arrived.

This afternoon Geeta and I went out wandering around Kara with our cameras—something I've meant to do in Lomé but never got around to. We talked with the dressmakers in Confiance Couture, a hairdresser and her customers, the server at a bar where we stopped for a Coke, a photographer who was thinking about repainting the mural on the front of his shop because, with the *crise économique*, he had little to do. He posed for a portrait with a portrait he'd taken of a man posing with a standing fan. Everyone was friendly and pleased to be photographed. It seemed so easy to talk with people with whom we shared a language and an urban life.

It's been a great trip. When we left, Nick and Geeta were mired in the bureaucracy of leaving, the motif of which is that nothing is possible. No exit permit without a *quitus*, no *quitus* without certificates that utility bills have been paid, no certificates without closing the accounts—in short, no water or electricity for some long time before leaving. But out on the road, everything is possible. We could go anywhere, talk to anybody, handle any surprise—because "everything is possible" has that sense, too, as well as the sense that the country is accommodating and that we feel capable. It's true that we couldn't communicate in the Tamberma village, but even the fact that we could go there and encounter the barrier is amazing. On the way back to the hotel from town this afternoon, Geeta and I met a boy who proudly identified us as *touristes*. We cried in unison, "Non! Pas touristes! Nous habitons Lomé!" But then we realized, anyone climbing back up the hill to the Hotel Kara was a tourist. And there's a great freedom tourists have that residents don't have, that even we don't have in Lomé.

The Color Purple
✉ ✉ ✉ ✉ ✉ ✉

I've been working the last few weeks on an unforeseen project. I gave Vera a copy of *The Color Purple* for Christmas, and she mentioned later that she'd enjoyed it and passed it on to her aunt, who had retold the story in Mina to her sister and niece in their regular Wednesday afternoon storytelling sessions, and they had liked it, too. The aunt, Davi, was educated in Ghana so reads English, but her sister, Amano, speaks only Mina and doesn't read at all.

I was astonished. We American feminist academics seize a book like *The Color Purple*, devour it, teach it, analyze it, praise it, but unconsciously translate it into terms that connect with our own lives. We may not wonder how it would strike a reader whose life was like that of Celie, the abused black country girl–then–woman who writes letters to God because she can't communicate her pain to people. Or if we do wonder, we don't know any women like this to ask. They're not in our classes and they're probably not reading novels. Only a few of us could come as close as the grandmother who was Alice Walker's inspiration. And though we talk about the vernacular language of Celie's letters, we approach it as a departure from standard literary English. We finesse the fact that Celie is "writing" in a language in which there's nothing to read; we don't know what it's like to have only an oral language. Amano was a "reader" who was like Celie at least in her relationship to language.

I asked Vera if I could go to the storytelling meeting sometime and talk with Davi, Amano, and Amano's daughter Juliette about the novel. There were so many things I wanted to know. The most problematic aspect of the novel, for me, is its portrayal of Africa, where Celie's sister goes with a missionary couple. Here was a chance to ask African women what they thought of it. But most important, the novel upsets a lot of traditional assumptions about sex, gender, and family relations and replaces them with new possibilities. Some of the revolutionary result is traditional in Africa, for example, that the multiple sexual partners of one man can cooperate with each other and regard each other's children as their own. But most of it violates tenaciously held traditions, for example, that *women* can have multiple sexual partners, and of both sexes, or that women can have careers and men take care of home and children. Most women in Togo both support their children and serve their husbands. I remembered René insisting that homosexuality didn't exist. Women don't even wear pants. It would be fascinating to talk about all this with African women.

Vera reported that her aunts liked the idea of talking with me, and we met three weeks ago at Davi's. I should mention that "Davi" and "Amano" are terms of relationship. After some initial confusion over what I should call Vera's aunts, they asked me to address them as Vera does. "Davi" means "little older sister," the name Vera picked up from her mother. "Amano" means "mother of Ama," the name for a girl born on Saturday. Looking at them, you wouldn't guess that Davi and Amano are sisters. Vera calls Davi "the American lady," says she's picked up American style from visiting her daughter in Virginia. And Vera's right. Tall, well-corseted, in a flower-sprigged summer Sunday dress, Davi could be a rather conservative American matron. When I took a group photograph, she looked directly and questioningly into the camera. Amano is shorter and heavier than Davi and was wearing the typical Togolese housedress of blouse and *pagne* in dark muddy colors. Her eyes had the look of hiding behind something. The two women seemed to embody the differences between Ghanaian and Togolese upbringing and between education and tradition.

Our visit was pleasant but frustrating. I explained that I wanted to tape the conversation so I could share their responses to the novel with American readers, at least in my classes and possibly in an article, and none of them seemed bothered by the tape recorder. But there was the problem of language. I thought I'd speak English with Davi and French with Juliette, a *lycée* student, and Vera would interpret between Amano and me. But Juliette was shy about using her French, and Davi is more comfortable reading than speaking English, so before long, Vera was leading the others in a discussion in Mina and then reporting the gist to me in English. Then there was the familiar chasm between the literary critic who thinks about the implications of plot, character, and style and readers who just enjoy the story. And in addition, there was the fact that I was a stranger and a white woman asking about fairly sensitive issues.

I tried first to find out *how* Davi had told the story. Had she told it as it's written in the form of letters spoken by Celie? Davi said, "I just told the story." Did she try to convey in Mina the fact that Celie's language was not standard English? Did she indicate that there was a difference between Celie's language and Nettie's? She said no. Davi didn't understand my questions about form, and I didn't understand then that Mina *is* a "nonstandard" dialect in the sense that it is a strictly oral vernacular, the written counterpart of which is Ewe. My student Améyou realized as we discussed this later that the relationship between Mina and Ewe is comparable to that between black and standard English. Davi didn't have to do anything to the language to make it correspond to Celie's. Though she found reading nonstandard English difficult at first, Mina was for her, as black vernacular for Celie, neither standard nor nonstandard, just language.

I enlisted Améyou to translate the Mina on the tapes for me because when I started transcribing them I noticed that Vera's summaries of long interchanges in Mina were remarkably short. The translation revealed that there was a lot going on I hadn't known at the time. Vera embellished and sometimes changed the meaning of my questions. For example, when I asked if they thought the portrayal of the Africans in the novel seemed right, Vera said, "What do you think of those men in the village who didn't do anything when their houses were demolished?" She also tidied up and filled in the responses with her own views. And with a simultaneous translation of the Mina I could tell what provoked Amano's and Davi's laughter. I thought they didn't see the sexual aspect of Celie and Shug's friendship. The context of a laugh showed that they did.

So between the natural meanderings of a conversation, the interruptions as other family members came and went through the enclosed front porch where we were sitting, the conflicting assumptions of the several participants, and the multiple layers of translation, the whole experience was pretty confusing. I'm only now sorting it out and seeing that Amano changed in the course of the conversation and that she, Davi, and Vera are very different kinds of readers.

What Davi, Amano, and Juliette all liked about the novel was the happy ending, the fact that a generation later Celie is united with the children taken from her at birth. Juliette also liked the fact that the missionary wife apologized to Nettie for being unkind to her when she thought Nettie was taking her husband. Amano said she never believed the story would end happily; she thought Celie would never see her children again.

Vera asked, "If you agree with me that things don't happen like that in real life, why does Alice Walker make it happen that way?"

"How can I know?" asked Amano. "This is too big a question for me to answer. I'm not Alice Walker."

Vera pushed, and Amano conceded, "Well, it's to teach something."

"Okay," said Vera, slipping easily into the probing professorial mode, "to teach what?"

Amano resisted: "This is like you. I give you an answer and you come with more questions. It's just one of God's miracles."

I asked if they thought Celie herself had changed as well as her circumstances. "Is Celie at the end, sitting on the porch, sewing pants, telling Albert she doesn't need him as a husband, the same Celie who let her father and Albert and Harpo walk all over her at the beginning?"

Amano replied, in Vera's translation, "From the beginning, Celie put herself to be a humble person, patient. If she hadn't had that character, if she'd been jealous and nasty to her, Shug wouldn't have taken to her and tried to help, and she'd have still been the same Celie right to the end. It's her humbleness that raised her up."

Améyou pointed out that the word Vera translated as *humble* also meant "kindhearted" or "having the disposition to do something good for people regardless of what they deserve." Thus Amano was implying that Celie is rewarded for acting without regard to reward, and the reward is coming not from Shug but from God.

"What then did you think of Shug?" I asked. "She wasn't humble, was she?"

"I don't think anything of her," Amano replied. "Shug is Shug. She is thoughtless. She takes what she wants. We all know that. That's the definition of Shug. She's a woman of bad life." Everybody laughed.

"Well, then," asked Vera, "how do you explain the friendship that develops between Celie and Shug, knowing each for what she is?"

"Here's another big question," Amano said again. "At first, Shug was very abusive toward Celie, and then later on, she realized that in spite of her nastiness, it wasn't having any effect. Celie was still being attentive toward her and helping her get better. That was what made her change and start looking more toward Celie to see what she could do to help."

What Davi, Juliette, and especially Amano found in *The Color Purple* was not a challenge to their social ideas but reinforcement of their hope that through their own humility the abused and oppressed would eventually be raised up. They considered Celie, not Shug, the agent of change in the novel, and her humility not an initial liability but a constant strength.

At the same time, it seemed to emerge that Amano had gotten from the novel encouragement to be less humble. I tried to pursue the question of revolutionary ideas. "Shug introduces Celie to some new ideas, for example, that women can wear pants, that women can be lovers to each other, that God is an It. Are these new ideas good for Celie?"

"Yes," said Amano, readily. The telling laugh had come when Vera translated the phrase about women being lovers to each other. Vera omitted the example of God being an It, Améyou said, perhaps because there is no gender distinction among pronouns in Mina and the pronoun would not be used for God anyway. So our discussion stuck to gender roles. "Shug opened Celie's eyes, and that's good. Doing that helped Celie to become a person."

Vera interjected: "It's very good. Because it stops Celie from thinking all you have to do is to serve a man, cook his food, make his clothes, wash his clothes, and just generally be a servant."

Davi agreed: "Until Shug came, all Celie knew was to be a *boy-vi*. But then when Shug came and introduced these new ideas, her eyes were opened."

"Do you think Shug is an eye-opener to the people reading the novel as well?" I asked.

"Yes," said Amano.

"How?" asked Vera. Amano and Davi laughed.

"The book does open the eyes of the reader," Amano said. "If I go somewhere, I learn something. I will use what I learned somewhere else. I might see someone helpless, someone left out. Maybe their peers made it, but they didn't, because they were unlucky. Now I know that such things are possible, and I will use that if I go anywhere."

"What Amano means," explained Davi, "is that if someday she happens to see such things happening to somebody, she will remember what happened to Celie and how she dealt with those things."

"Is it likely," I asked, "that she would find somebody in Celie's situation?"

They all laughed. "Oh, yes," said Vera, "there are people."

Although Amano kept repeating at first that the questions we asked were too big for her, I noticed that she was the one who offered the most substantial comments. And as the discussion developed, she stopped demurring, became involved, asked questions of her own.

When I asked if there was anything about the novel the others found hard to understand or accept, Davi asked why it was that Sophia learned to drive and the mayor's wife couldn't learn and became so dependent on her. She was an outsider puzzled by the social context of the story.

But Amano's question came from Celie's point of view: "Throughout the whole story there was something I couldn't accept, something strange, something I couldn't believe—that was how a father could have sex with his own daughter. Then when we learned that he wasn't the real father, it wasn't quite so bad. But, even then, it's not right. You don't do that."

When Vera asked what they thought of the men in the African village who didn't do anything when their houses were demolished, Amano leapt to react: "When did you ever see people watching their houses being demolished and not doing anything about it? I can't see how that could be done, that they would decide to make a road go through your house without telling you. This is bad. You would be in your house and they would come and demolish your house without telling you anything? Even here, they wouldn't make a road go through your house without telling you. You might not agree with it, but they would tell you."

"Well," asked Vera, "what do you think of the education they give their children?"

Davi said, "Remember what we were told when Tashi was doing well in school? That her father didn't want her to go any further? The people didn't want their children to go to school because they were a backward people and wanted their children to remain as backward as they themselves were."

"But they allowed their sons to go to school," Vera pointed out.

Again, it was Amano who reacted sharply: "Why didn't they want to send the girls to school? What have the girls done not to be sent to school? What are they being punished for?"

"That's what I'm asking you."

"That's what I'm asking *you*, too!"

"How is it," I asked Vera on the way home, "that Amano's older sister got an education, and she didn't?"

"Oh," said Vera, "when Amano was talking about someone being left out and unlucky, she was talking about herself. She has had a very hard life. When my grandmother died, my mother was in boarding school in Cape Coast; Davi had already graduated and was about to be married; and the two brothers—I'm not sure just where they were, but they were old enough to look after themselves, or help my grandfather on the farm or something. But Amano was only about ten, and my grandfather didn't think he could look after a little girl, so he sent her to my grandmother's sister in Kpalimé. That wasn't very far away, but it was across the border, because they were living near Ho in the British part of Togo, and of course

Kpalimé was in the French part. So Amano had started school in English, and then she had to switch to French. And whether because of that, or losing her mother at just that age, or what, she didn't do well, didn't get on. And her aunt was a bit old, and maybe not too capable of handling a young girl, and one thing led to another, and the result was that Amano was married very young, fifteen or something.

"And she wasn't lucky in a man. Her husband is very demanding—gets angry if the meal he fancies isn't ready when he happens to come home, which could be anytime, because he comes and goes just as he pleases. He's just nasty to Amano and never paid any attention to his children, except maybe to hit them. He's got another wife and a couple of kids over in Bé; Amano pretends not to know, but she does. He doesn't give her much money, just enough so she can't leave him, because what could she do to get enough money to take care of a family? She's one of those people, like I said, who's dependent, so she has to be extra humble so she can survive. It's getting a little better now. Juliette's her last child, and I think one or two of the older ones are helping her out so she's not so dependent on her husband."

As Améyou and I went over the tapes, I realized that Vera, Davi, and Amano had read *The Color Purple* very differently. Vera, like me, had organized her reading into concepts and, with the instincts of a professor, tried to fit others' responses into the same concepts. Davi was interested in the characters as people, but other people; for her the story remained a story. Amano stepped inside the story; she *was* Celie when Celie was abused; she *was* Tashi when Tashi was pulled out of school. It was Amano, the illiterate, to whom the novel was life.

"I know Amano," Améyou said when I told him her story. "I mean, not Amano specifically, but I *know* her. She could be my mother. She wants to believe everything is the way it's supposed to be, because she's been brought up to believe that if you're good, everything will be okay. So if everything is okay, it means she's good, which she knows she is. But deep down, she knows everything isn't okay. This book is tough."

I feel I've come to know Amano a little, too. But only a little. And that little has taken so much—the unlikely catalyst of a novel in common, professorial persistence, a tape recorder, two translators, and time. And it seems out of sync, like a satellite telephone call, to come to that feeling of recognition now with Améyou and not three weeks ago with Amano.

Borders
⊠ ⊠ ⊠

It looks as though Vera and I will go to Accra next week.

The Ghana border has been closed all year. Ghana keeps closing it in an effort to keep its cocoa farmers from smuggling cocoa into Togo, where they can get a better price for it, in hard currency, than they could by selling it to the Ghana Cocoa Board and letting the government take the profit and the foreign exchange.

The border makes living in Lomé like living at the edge of a cliff. It runs right past Kodjoviakopé, the pleasant diplomatic neighborhood where Kay lives, but I haven't actually seen it except from a distance. Nick walked over there one evening out of curiosity and got a gun held on him. More than threat the border poses mystery: What's happening in Ghana? The Ghanaian newspapers hawked in the Lomé cafés don't tell you anything important. And when embassy people go to Accra they stay in the diplomatic cocoon and don't learn what life is like for either ordinary Ghanaians or unofficial travelers. I asked a Peace Corps volunteer who had been sent to Accra for dental work what it was like. He said he'd felt uncomfortable, but he hadn't ventured far enough from the Peace Corps office and the hotel pool to learn anything very specific. Oddly, we consider Accra the site of both safe medicine and vague danger.

The border is different for Africans—at least some of them. I've heard stories that Ghanaian schoolchildren who live right on the border climb over their back walls every day to go to school in Togo and return with pockets full of soap and batteries from the Lomé market. Mercy went through the bush to visit her mother in Ghana. My student Ms. Agbodo retrieved her stolen motorcycle across the border, where the Ghana police had impounded it. Lately it seems that the Togolese are no longer bothering to cross through the bush; the price of an unofficial crossing right in Lomé has become fixed—a thousand francs for the Togolese guards, a thousand for the Ghanaians, free same-day return.

It's only the road border that's closed, so for people who can afford to fly, it's an inconvenience but not a barrier. Vera's father, who works for an international relief agency, has come to Lomé on business two or three times this year. He admits that it's cheaper to come by road and easier to take back supplies, but since he can still visit Vera and his mother, who also lives in Lomé, he's not seriously upset. He seems to regard the border closing as a sad thing for international relations but a temporary and tolerable aggravation in his own life. For someone like Vera, though, who is too highly placed to cross the border illegally but can't afford plane travel, the border is a real barrier. When she went home in November for her brother's wedding, it was a big deal. Philippe, who as an ECOWAS officer (and a Togolese) considers the border closing a violation by Ghana of international agreement, refused to go himself. Only at the last minute did they decide they could afford to send Vera. Then space had to be found on the flight and a friend of a relative enlisted to expedite the exit permit. Vera couldn't inform her parents she was coming, because of course there's no telephone connection between Togo and Ghana, nor could she call them from the Accra airport, because the phones don't work within Accra either, so it was just intuition that made her father stop by the airport that afternoon to see if she'd arrived. A trip of 125 miles was a major undertaking.

For months Vera has been asking me when I'm going to Accra. But I haven't wanted to go without her, and we haven't both been free until now. Vera just quit the job she's been unhappy with all year, and the final English Department meeting has been set for Friday. It's understood that I pay for the plane tickets and Vera's family provides hospitality. The only question is whether Vera can find someone to stay in her house, which she is afraid to leave empty. Philippe won't be back from a trip up north till after we've left; Mercy has finally accepted a live-in job; and Vera doesn't trust her maid to know who should and shouldn't be let into the house.

One reason Ghana intrigues me is a remark Vera's father made on a visit to Lomé. "Even though I have family here," he said, "I'm always glad to get back to Accra." Why, I asked. "Because I feel freer," he said.

The Airport

✉ ✉ ✉ ✉ ✉

Last night after the department meeting I picked up Britt and Amy and went to the airport to see off Kay, leaving Togo for good, and the students going to the U.S. to be camp counselors. The Peace Corps director was going back, too, accompanying the body of a volunteer murdered this week. The camp counselors included my friends Améyou and Ajavon; most of the rest of my students were there seeing off their friends. Alidou and his friend Charles were there for some of the camp counselors and especially for the murdered volunteer, who was a friend of theirs. A lot of the Cultural Center staff was there for Kay, including Albert, the driver, who stood in the background behind his ever-present shades and didn't say a thing but stayed till the plane took off. Most of us had several people to say good-bye to. Simon Amégavie ran back and forth among the group around Kay, the camp counselors, whom he's responsible for, and his family, since one of the counselors is his daughter.

A moment like this makes Lomé seem like a college campus, where "everybody" leaves for the summer. I'm glad I'm not going just yet. It also dramatizes how small and interconnected my world here is. And how central is the airport to foreigners and the few Togolese who will escape the limits of a small Third World country. After the plane took off, as the crowd descended from the observation deck, an elderly woman in *pagne* and head tie walked into the glass door. Most people don't escape.

The murder of the volunteer shocked everybody. I heard about it first from Alidou and Charles when they came to my house to pick up the radio Charles is buying from me. They are devastated. They feel grief because she was a friend and guilt that Togo did it to her. Some of the Americans are doubly shocked because they believed Togo was not a violent society. It is violent, though. Wife and child abuse are common, and the belief that misfortune is caused by another person's malevolence leads to chains of revenge. It's just that foreigners are not usually the victims of the violence. In this case, domestic abuse, revenge, and cross-cultural misunderstanding converged. According to the story being pieced together, the volunteer discovered that the teenage girl helping her with housework was stealing. Thinking to help rather than punish, she went to the girl's father, who then beat his daughter brutally. The girl took revenge on the one she considered the cause of her injury. The presence of Alidou and Charles in my living room grieving over the death of an American reflected the bonds that have developed this year; the murder itself reflects all the missed connections.

A few weeks ago, I had a dream that a whole group of Americans decided to go home. We walked a long time through woods to a train. When we finally got to the train, I suddenly wondered why I'd left—I had so much more to do in Togo. When I told the dream to Amy, she said she'd had the same one: on a plane, seized with regret for leaving.

Isabella Bird has just told me one reason I'm leaving. The small, interconnected community is just too small. One of the things I've been doing toward packing up is to read some of the books I brought to fill the long lonely hours that haven't materialized—currently, *Six Months in the Sandwich Islands*, Isabella Bird's letters to her sister in Glasgow from her visit to Hawaii in 1873. When the sister, evidently impressed with the paradise Isabella had been describing, proposed to come out and join her, Isabella fired back a reply giving the reasons she herself was leaving for the Rocky Mountains. The first was *nuhou*, gossip. When I read her description of "the perpetual talking about people, and the picking to tatters of every item of personal detail, whether gathered from fact or imagination," I thought she had to have been listening in on the endless speculation about who doesn't get along with whom at the American School, what the Cultural Center director has against Kay, whom René's been seen with, whether Monette will last in Togo, why the new couple is so standoffish. I didn't realize till I read Isabella that this pettiness isn't unique to Lomé but characteristic of the small foreign community. It's the flip side of the "intimate friendly relations" that make the community so appealing. But it's also inexorable: "You can hardly be long here without being drawn into its vortex." Debilitating: "Over-indulgence in it destroys the privacy of individual existence, and is deteriorating in more ways than one." And, especially, frustrating: "The ingenuity with which *nuhou* is circulated is worthy of a better cause." The better cause that we're all supposedly here to do.

The good part of the small, interconnected world is the interconnectedness: the way Togolese and Americans meet at the airport for a community send-off; the way Amy and Rama can meet in SGGG and join forces to help their classmate from Chad; the way black, white, and *métisse* children form big frisbee games in the Sarakawa pool; the way their French, German, and American mothers meet and gab in whichever is the common language of the group; the way, freed from our own cultures, black and white Americans, U.S. Americans and Québecois, North Americans and Russians, form new alliances and identities. But all the cosmopolitanness that makes Lomé exciting comes from the same thing that makes it uncomfortable—poverty. It's the fact that Togo is a poor country that brings aid workers from all over the world, creates the international atmosphere, and supports the restaurants, cultural centers, and supermarkets where we meet. There's no relationship—between teacher and student, between American and Togolese colleagues, between expatriates—that doesn't derive from the national and racial distinction between having and not having. And there's no gesture of the day that doesn't reflect it. Buying bread, taking out the garbage, getting into the freshly washed car, stopping at a light. When I go to the Sarakawa pool with Lee Ann and her kids, we spend about 4,000 francs to get in, while the guy who brings us pads for the lounge chairs probably makes 1,000 a day. What I'm looking forward to most in going home is being simply myself, not a *yovo*, not a fine lady, not a representative of the privileges to which others aspire. Of course, going home doesn't change the basic relationship. It only puts it farther away.

A Day on the Ghana Border

⊠ ⊠ ⊠ ⊠ ⊠ ⊠ ⊠ ⊠ ⊠

Vera and I are sitting in the bus station on the Ghana side of the border wondering what's happened to our ride to Accra.

Last Thursday, Ghana opened the border. I called on Vera and we discussed driving to Accra, but I didn't trust the border to stay open till we came back, and besides, said Vera, "there are bound to be a lot of checkpoints on the road, and after all this time without traffic from Togo the soldiers will be very hungry." So we decided to fly as planned on Sunday.

Then on Friday I got a message at the Cultural Center to stop by Vera's again. She'd had a message that her father's assistant, Moses, was in Lomé to pick up a van the relief agency had had delivered to the port and been unable to collect while the border was closed. If we waited till today, we could ride with Moses—and he could deal with the hungry soldiers.

We arranged to meet Moses here about noon, as he has to take the van across the border empty. We took a taxi from Vera's grandmother's house to the border and walked across. Vera brought along her fifteen-year-old cousin Kweku to help with our luggage, which includes, besides commodities unavailable or expensive in Ghana, a big bag of fried turkey tails sent by Vera's grandmother.

"The border" is just a collection of sheds on a rutted dusty road. I wouldn't have known where to go, but Vera did. The Togolese officials were casual and jolly. As soon as we passed to the Ghana side, we could feel a difference. Tough-looking women in army fatigues demanded that we hand over our wallets. We understood that this was for the currency declaration, but there was an element of hold-up in the demand, too. Vera got up on her high horse and told them she had been in the army, too, and that was no way to treat a sister officer. That got us through immigration, and we proceeded to the customs shed.

The customs officers wanted to unpack and stamp every bag of sugar and bar of soap we were taking to Vera's family. This would give them the opportunity to pocket a few, as they tried to do with Vera's. I had made a list of all the items in my bag of commissary goodies and asked them to stamp that instead because the bag was so carefully packed. The word went down the line to accommodate the white lady. The officer copied my list over, stopping at "cake mix," "pudding mix," and "couscous" to ask "What's that?" and have me show it. Then he stamped the list. The stamps supposedly allow us to take the goods through the checkpoints we'll encounter on the road. As we finished, the men said, "Now, your CFA coins."

"What?" we asked.

"For beer—not all you have, just enough for beer."

Meanwhile, nobody questioned Kweku, who is carrying no papers at all.

There was no new van parked over here when we got through customs. We've now been waiting about three hours. Two hours ago, Vera sent Kweku back to Lomé to find out what happened to Moses. Now we're wondering what's happened to him as well. We can't go back without forfeiting my visa, but by now we can't make it to Accra before dark.

The bus station is nothing but a concrete platform with a few broken benches, a closed ticket window with a chalked schedule, and a roof. Behind the station is a strip of dirty sand and the ocean. There are no toilet facilities. The air smells of salt and shit. Across the street, harlequin-patched taxis with names like "My Lord Only" and "Who Knows Tomorrow Mama?" pull in and depart every few minutes. One labeled "Good God Clinic" keeps returning. When a taxi is ready to depart, three or four men hanging around give it a push.

At two o'clock, after the noon bus departed, we got seats on the platform. Until then, we sat on the edge, next to a pile of twenty-five-liter cans of vegetable oil and big coils of rubber-coated wire, trying to keep within the shade of the roof. Passengers are beginning to accumulate now for the next bus. Two little girls, just steady on their feet, have been playing for the last half hour with the two parts of a Winston cigarette package on the floor. Already they have the pout and the sway-hipped walk of their wax print–wrapped mothers. A woman has set up a cook stand in front of the station. When she tossed out a basin of water, a yellow dog raced to lick up the puddle. A little boy with her is scrubbing an aluminum kettle with a rag and sand.

I took a short walk back toward the border. Along the sea side of the road are low shacks housing customs expediters, including the Smooth Way Cargo Traffic Agency. An arch in the shape of a ceremonial stool straddles the border and tells travelers leaving Ghana, "Bye-Bye Safe Journey." The men sitting in front of Nkuabia's Glory Enterprises and the women across the road selling cassava balls and sugarcane from basins on the ground kept track of my progress.

We thought we were being foresighted to bring along boiled eggs, peanuts, and oranges to eat in the van, but they turned out to be less than a lunch. We've been thirsty all afternoon. We counted on the water Moses is carrying in the van. A few hundred yards away on the Togo side of the arch, vendors are selling bottled drinks and oranges. Here there is nothing to drink except iced water from a stand prophetically called "Thy Kingdom Come."

When a coconut vendor appeared we felt like desert travelers spotting an oasis—even though I don't like the thin, slightly acidic milk of green coconuts and she charged us double because we had CFA instead of cedis. Her baby's head bobbled on her back as she whacked off the tops of the coconuts with her *coupe-coupe*. When we'd drained the milk, we copied the other customers and took the husks back to the vendor, who whacked them in half so we could scoop up the meat, like raw egg white, using the tops as spoons.

Then Vera said, "Well, I'm not going to sit here and starve while I look after a bag of turkey tails. They'll probably be spoiled by the time we get to Accra, anyway." I've seen fried turkey tails for sale on the street in Lomé. Fist-sized blobs of fat—they must come from sixty-pound turkeys (the same ones whose hefty thighs and drumsticks are sold as parts in American supermarkets?). Two things I thought I'd never do: eat turkey tails and pee on the beach.

Evening

Kweku returned about 4:30. He'd found Moses at Vera's grandmother's (and stayed to lunch). The one and only man who could release the van at the port was not there this morning, so Moses had to wait until after lunch, that is, three o'clock, to begin to get the van. He didn't get to the border till nearly dark, too late to clear the van today, but he persuaded the officials to let him drive through and take us to a hotel and return in the morning to clear customs.

We're now in a derelict hotel about ten miles from the border. It must have once been a popular resort. It has several buildings linked by overgrown gravel walks. I don't have much sense of the layout, as we arrived in the dark, in a downpour. Vera and I were put in one building, Moses in another, although it's hard to believe there are any guests filling the other rooms in either building. We expected to join Moses for supper, but since supper was brought to our room, we haven't seen him since we arrived. We don't even know exactly where he is.

Our room is large and dusty, with blue walls, a splintery dresser, and a single fluorescent tube whose switch is beside the door. Vera immediately made sure the door locked. The mosquito nets are gray, with some patches and some holes. Supper was a plate of rice with fiery sauce. I could only eat the rice by scraping off as much as possible of the sauce. The only bottled beverage available is beer; it helped wash down the pepper, but aggravated the dehydration. We're now gratefully chugging iodine-flavored water for which we've waited two hours—first till the young woman attending us brought dinner so we could ask her for empty bottles in which to treat the water, then till she brought the bottles, then till the water purification tablets worked.

Our attendant, who has now taken away the dinner dishes and brought galvanized pails of hot water, couldn't be nicer. She acts as though fetching and carrying down a long gravel path in the rain is her great privilege. But we have an odd sense of being confined in a remote fastness on a dark and stormy night.

Accra and Home
✉ ✉ ✉ ✉ ✉ ✉

We finally left the border at mid-morning Wednesday and arrived in Accra in mid-afternoon—five hours for 125 miles. The road was ragged with potholes, and we were stopped at twelve checkpoints. A customs officer hitched a ride with us. He got free transportation; we got some protection against harassment. Even so, at one checkpoint, a policeman made trouble about insurance for the passengers "if something happens." He was drunk, and the customs officer condemned him roundly, but only to us, for "making a fool of himself in front of his own people." From Tema to Accra, we followed a bus with bags of powdered milk piled on the roof rack and boys with white-smeared mouths hanging off the back. We snacked from roadside stands along the way, dropping the fried bean balls in our laps and dribbling mango juice down our fronts as the van swerved and bounced around and through the potholes.

When we got to Vera's father's office in downtown Accra, hot, jarred, sticky, and from our point of view a day late, we felt we'd heroically completed a difficult quest. Vera's father said, "You should have let us know you were coming."

On the way to Vera's parents' house on the outskirts of Accra, we passed many half-built houses whose owners don't have the money to finish them. The Akollys' house is on a wide puddle-pocked dirt street in a treeless neighborhood of raw cinder-block walls, garbage piles, and foraging chickens.

Inside the gate, however, the whole atmosphere was transformed. We were in an orderly, patriarchal, British-colonial household impervious to the chaos without. The man who ran to open the gate had been watering the flower beds; the house was spread out, sparely furnished, cool, calm. Vera and I were shown to separate guest rooms, each with a bath, all made up. There was another guest, a colleague of Mr. Akolly's from Sierra Leone. After Vera and I cleaned up, she went to gossip with her mother in the kitchen, and I sat with Mr. Akolly and his colleague and talked West African politics and development until dinner. Ghana has been in terrible economic straits for the last half-dozen years. When I was in Accra in 1978, the shelves in the grocery section of Kingsway were empty except for a few cans of Campbell's soup priced like caviar and spaced about a foot apart. You had to know someone to buy meat, and even local produce like bananas was hard to find in the market. The cocoa smuggling that keeps closing the Ghana-Togo border is both a result of inflation and a cause of further inflation. And one reason we now have pretty reliable electricity in Togo is that it comes from Ghana, which needs foreign exchange so badly it prefers to sell the power to Togo and run short at home. Mr. Akolly is serenely sanguine about Ghana's present situation. He thinks the austerity measures President Rawlings has imposed to reduce consumption of imports and support Ghana's own production are already working.

In the morning, one of the two nieces working as maids woke me up with "bed tea" and later brought me two buckets of water, hot and cold, for a bath. The tub had faucets, but the water was off, as usual. The bath water came from a well; drinking water is purchased. The family sat down together to a breakfast served in courses—porridge, fried eggs and sausage, toast and tea. Mr. Akolly shook his newspaper and fussed that Vera was late.

When we went out no one but me seemed to notice that everything was topsy-turvy. One of Vera's brothers, delighted at the distraction we offered, volunteered to drive us around. We couldn't go very far because one of the austerity measures is gas rationing. You can only buy gas on odd or even dates according to your license plate number and then only in small quantities. So when we arrived unexpectedly, the tank in the family's second car was nearly empty, and it was the wrong day to put gas in it. No problem. Reggie just walked around to the back of the gas station, paid a little more, and got the gas in a can. We attended a parade at the military hospital where Vera trained. The festive pomp of bands, fancy maneuvers, horsemanship, and speeches clashed with the wards I saw later, where there were big holes in the screens and no soap to wash the floors. Mostly, we made the rounds of Vera's aunts and cousins, who talked of the things relatives talk of everywhere—new babies, illnesses, and who said what to whom. I never got to see how the shelves of Kingsway look now, because

Vera wasn't interested. I didn't learn until just before we left what everyone else of course knew all along, that Reggie is a schoolteacher who skipped school to drive us around.

The only people who seemed to feel something was wrong were the couple who own the design agency Vera's brother Stephen, whom I met in Lomé, works for. They'd been without water for two weeks while pipes on their street were being sporadically replaced. Their business depends on contracts from Togo and the Ivory Coast because Ghanaian businesses can't afford anything so intangible as design, and border closings and poor communications make foreign business difficult. The wife said she not only couldn't afford to serve her family meat, she couldn't even afford peanut soup anymore. They couldn't imagine how they were going to educate their children to the level they'd achieved. The husband didn't think the austerity measures would work, because no regulations can be tight enough to prevent Ghanaians from getting around them.

One result of Vera's success with the women soldiers at the border was that we didn't have currency declaration forms, without which it is supposed to be impossible to get out of Ghana. But at the airport, Mr. Akolly fixed that up. Reggie took our tickets and elbowed through the mob at the check-in desk to get our boarding passes and carried our suitcases past the "passengers only" point almost to the gate.

When we arrived in the Lomé airport, the world seemed to have turned suddenly rational. The immigration officer said "Bonne arrivée" as he stamped our passports; the customs inspector checked our bags briskly.

Britt and Amy and Philippe were there to meet us, and we all went to Keur Rama for lunch. The dining room was full of French and Togolese families out for Sunday dinner. Rama herself, who recognizes us by now, came over to say *bonjour*. It was so comfortable there recounting our adventures to Britt and Amy and Philippe, it was painfully like coming home.

Postscript, 1991

I've been back to Togo twice in the last year. In August 1990 I went to visit friends and to see how closely the Togo I'd written about resembled the one I'd see now. In January 1991 I returned with a student group on a West African study tour.

In August, little had changed in Lomé. A peace dove had been erected in the center of the Rond Point, and the taxi station and market there had been moved. Two new supermarkets had opened and a few public telephone booths been installed. Foreign companies had taken over and reopened a number of factories. Industrial building was spreading out from the port and pushing the beach farther east. There were probably more jobs in Lomé, but the people I talked to said that wages had stayed the same while prices went up, and it was harder than ever to get by. The vision that struck me hardest as Lee Ann drove me home from the airport was the familiar and terrifying yellow fog on unpaved roads at night which obscured the bicycles lurching around holes into traffic. I'd become too used to it when I lived there to grasp its symbolic force.

The biggest difference in my view of Lomé resulted from my own changed vantage point. I was closer to my Togolese friends this time— partly because we had corresponded for six years, partly just because I had come back—and I felt their frustration. Mahouna had opened his *boutique* but still depended on his housekeeper's wages to keep it going and didn't yet have a housekeeping job for the coming school year. Elise showed me extensive new building at the university but said that, though enrollment had doubled in six years, neither the size of the faculty nor faculty salaries had increased. She'd been promoted but had not received even a cost-of-living raise. She was doing more work for less pay.

Alidou, who had kept a professional distance while he was my French tutor in Togo, had written me regularly since I'd left. He had found a government job and married his childhood sweetheart. They'd had a son, brought to live with them an older son he'd never mentioned before, and started to build a house. He seemed to have made it. But Alidou had worked with Peace Corps volunteers. He had shelves full of books and cassettes volunteers had given him and a notebook full of their addresses. He wanted the mobility and adventure of the Americans he'd trained. The job that had been so difficult to get would never involve travel, offered little scope for advancement, and only just allowed him to build his house, one course of cinder blocks at a time. At thirty-five, he'd transferred his dreams of a wider life to his fifteen-year-old son.

My former student Améyou, friend now after years of holiday visits while he studied in the States, had recently returned to Togo after several years abroad. He had always chafed against the limitations of life in Togo—worn shorts to class, for example: "Why not? It's hot." Now that he'd made his own way in both America and Europe, he was frustrated that there seemed to be no way to integrate his experience into life in Togo. He felt his friends couldn't accept him as both Togolese and a citizen of a wider world. "You're back," they'd say. "I'm here," he'd reply.

I was often frustrated myself. I had luxuriously private guest quarters in a separate little house in Lee Ann's compound, with my own bathroom and terrace. But in an African household I was still caught up in the African web of interdependence I had escaped when I lived in my own apartment. Like most middle-class Togolese, Lee Ann had poor relations as household help. Her husband's twenty-five-year-old niece Dédé and two young girls, all abused or abandoned by their immediate families, lived in the *dépendance* and did the housework. *Dépendance* means outbuilding, but as it houses poor relations who work as servants it comes to represent the relationship between haves and have-nots in Africa. Energetic, egalitarian Lee Ann had become unconsciously dependent on Dédé, and as a guest dependent on Lee Ann, I had to depend on Dédé, too. When I asked for a rag to wipe up the water from my shower, Lee Ann said, "Dédé will do it." Eventually she did, but in the meantime I brushed my teeth standing in a puddle. When I picked up mosquito coils in SGGG, she said, "Let Dédé get those at the market." Mosquito coils were perhaps 25 francs cheaper in the neighborhood market, but we were in SGGG, and I didn't want to have to think about them again or to ask Dédé to walk a hot dusty mile to do what I could do without effort myself.

On the other hand, Dédé might have appreciated an excuse to go to the market because Lee Ann's husband wouldn't let her leave the compound except on errands. She got no salary, just presents and "anything she asked for," because, said Lee Ann, if she got regular pay, she would have to give it to her alcoholic father. Dédé had food, shelter, nice clothes, and appreciative employers but no freedom.

Améyou was trying to make his peace with Togo, Lee Ann was wondering about her future there, I was wondering whether I'd return. In long talks we probed our relationship to Africa. Lee Ann and I agreed that the great attraction of life in Lomé was freedom from barriers accepted at home. Here Lee Ann's children could be both Togolese and American, not, as in the United States, black or white. We could have friends of different nationalities and conversations in multiple languages. We could pick out what we liked of American, European, and African culture. We felt less American, more individual, more free.

But Dédé wasn't free. Mahouna and Elise were not free. The freedom of identity Lee Ann and I felt in Lomé was exactly what Alidou and Améyou craved but couldn't find. Even Lee Ann and I weren't free. She couldn't do without Dédé or pay her as she wanted to. I couldn't wipe up the puddle in my bathroom.

In each case this lack of freedom reflected the gulf between haves and have-nots in Africa. Améyou, who unlike Alidou had traveled but couldn't feel like himself in his own country, discovered this when he went out with me. One day we went to Togoville, a popular tourist destination partly because it is remote by road but easily accessible by pirogue. Améyou negotiated a round trip with the boatman, but when we showed up for the return trip, the boatman tried to increase the fare. Améyou was furious that a fellow Togolese would treat him as a tourist. But he seldom traveled with *yovos* or outside the circles frequented by students and professionals. To the boatman, he was not a fellow Togolese but one of the haves. Later, he took me to lunch at Marox Grill, a German restaurant in town popular with expatriates. There, although we understood that lunch was his treat, the waiter presented the bill to me. In Togoville, Améyou with me had been taken for a have; at Marox, for a have-not. The social barriers in Togo are relative; they don't necessarily coincide with race or nationality, but they're not down. The community of Europeans, Americans, and middle-class Togolese in Lomé is a community of haves in a country of have-nots.

In every encounter my pleasure in renewed ties was mixed with reminders of inequality.

In January, however, a great deal had changed. On October 5, students and others had rallied in support of people arrested for "disseminating tracts." On November 26, taxi drivers had struck to protest extortionate licensing and border-crossing fees. The government had sent out the army to put down "unrest," but it had also appointed a committee to draft a constitution and relinquished control of the press. When our study tour arrived in Lomé, half a dozen independent newspapers were reporting events and raising questions never touched by *La Nouvelle Marche*. The issues we saw printed the 1990 Amnesty International report on Togo, a pastoral letter from the Catholic bishops calling for political amnesty, and testimony of torture victims. The *Courrier du Golfe* published debate on the presidency of Sylvanus Olympio, whose overthrow in 1963 was being officially celebrated within the week. *Forum Hebdo* reported an army raid against a village that had tried to maintain its traditional right of way through the Marox ranch and questioned the relationship between Marox and the president. The papers satirized the government's suppression and distortion of information, printed and critiqued the draft constitution, and called for a nationally representative convention to revise it.

They pointed out the connection between poverty and dictatorship. A book review explained that Swiss prosperity was based in part on African poverty because Swiss banks helped dictators conceal public theft. A reply to a reader's letter asked how the press could discuss the national economy without inquiring into the discrepancy between a leader's expenditures and his salary as a public official.

They refused to be intimidated. The *Courrier du Golfe* reported on the front page that its editors had been summoned to court and those of *Forum Hebdo* charged with inciting revolt. They invited their readers to pack the courtroom and write letters in defense of a free press. They gave citizens a forum and apparently courage to speak up for their rights. The surveyors' association denounced government interference in the accreditation of surveyors. A student protested the presence of soldiers on the campus.

In Lomé there was an atmosphere of both tension and release. Tanks surveyed the January 13 parade route, and Togolese stayed off the streets at night. But for the first time in my experience, they talked politics. A former student of mine now employed in the planning ministry came to a lecture organized for our group on the tax-free zone being promoted by both the Togolese and American governments to attract foreign industry and create jobs. Afterward he argued against the zone because it would handicap Togolese businesses by giving foreigners the double advantage of cheap labor and tax relief and thus reinforce instead of relieve Togo's economic dependency. I asked whether he advanced this argument in the office. "Yes," he said, "we debate this all the time."

Alidou encouraged me most. He had never criticized the government, never associated his personal frustration with public policies, and always represented his job in an office that handled property disputes between the government and individuals as boring. When I asked him whether he ever challenged the government's position in these disputes, he said, "You know, I never did until now. I always thought the government represented the best interests of the people. But now I see they're not always right. And that it's important to look for disagreement. Now I ask the staff to suggest ways for the office to work better." Alidou was a new person. He had passed an exam and been promoted. He was writing a paper on land rights he hoped to get published and thinking of enrolling in a new doctoral program at the university. He wasn't making the money he would need to travel abroad, but he could see a future for himself in Lomé.

I don't know what I'll find the next time I go to Lomé, but now I expect change and hope that change will continue to shrink the gulf of inequality.